MW00748010

HIJACKED!
IDOLS IN DISGUISE

Breaking the stranglehold.
Falling in love with God again

ROSEMARY MONREAU

WESTBOW·
PRESS
A DIVISION OF THOMAS NELSON
& ZONDERVAN

Scripture quotations marked (ESV) are from the Holy Bible, English Standard Version˚ (ESV˚), copyright © 2001 by Crossway, a publishing ministry of Good News Publishers. Used by permission. All rights reserved.

Scripture quotations marked (NIV) are taken from the Holy Bible, New International Version®, NIV®. Copyright © 1973, 1978, 1984, 2011 by Biblica, Inc.™ Used by permission of Zondervan. All rights reserved worldwide. www.zondervan.com The "NIV" and "New International Version" are trademarks registered in the United States Patent and Trademark Office by Biblica, Inc.™

Scripture quotations marked (RSV) are from the Revised Standard Version of the Bible, copyright © 1946, 1952, and 1971 National Council of the Churches of Christ in the United States of America. Used by permission. All rights reserved.

Scripture quotations marked (NRSV) are from the New Revised Standard Version Bible, copyright © 1989 National Council of the Churches of Christ in the United States of America. Used by permission. All rights reserved.

Scripture taken from the New King James Version˚. Copyright © 1982 by Thomas Nelson. Used by permission. All rights reserved.

Scripture taken from The Holy Bible, 21ˢᵗ Century King James Version (KJ21˚), Copyright © 1994, Deuel Enterprises, Inc., Gary, SD 57237, and used by permission.

WestBow Press books may be ordered through booksellers or by contacting:

WestBow Press
A Division of Thomas Nelson & Zondervan
1663 Liberty Drive
Bloomington, IN 47403
www.westbowpress.com
1 (866) 928-1240

ISBN: 978-1-4908-5501-1 (sc)
ISBN: 978-1-4908-5502-8 (hc)
ISBN: 978-1-4908-5500-4 (e)

Library of Congress Control Number: 2014917689

Printed in the United States of America.

WestBow Press rev. date: 11/5/2014

CONTENTS

DEDICATION

To my children and grandchildren, praying that their lives will be full of the joy of the Lord and informed by God's guiding Word and wisdom.

ACKNOWLEDGEMENTS

This book would not have been possible without all the research it required; I wish to thank my alma mater, Regent College in Vancouver, British Columbia, for making their resources available during my residency and fieldwork. I thank Regent Faculty members, who generously gave of their time in discussing theological issues pertinent to everyday life and to the topic at hand. Particular thanks goes to Dr. John J. Stackhouse Sr. and Sangwoo Youtong Chee, professor of theology, for facilitating aspects of my residency and work. Heartfelt thanks, to those who were willing to share their personal stories in this book. My appreciation and thanks also go to Diane and Mary, who have provided feedback and critique, cheering me on along the way. Thank you, Guy-Michel and Audra, for critiquing and editing, and for your invaluable feedback.

PREFACE

Hijacked! *Idols in Disguise* explores the snares that have mesmerized and captivated Western Christians and offers a way to renewed freedom and courage. It is by no means exhaustive. Any mistakes in interpretation and explanation reside solely with the author. I invite you to join me on a journey that at times will feel very uncomfortable, at times maddening, maybe frightening. Most of all, my purpose is to engage us to reflect on why we might experience negative reactions as we read *Hijacked! Idols in Disguise*. An adverse response might be a sign that we need to transform our way of thinking and living in some areas of our lives. I wish to encourage each of us to keep an open mind as we travel together and explore what God may be saying to each of us. If tempted to say, "I have heard it all before," please listen again, but fully, that is, fully engaged with heart and mind and emotions and thus to *really* hear. In doing so I believe that you will hear beyond the words and into a small part of the heart of God. I say this with the utmost care and awe, being fully aware that none among us can possibly know the mind of God, at least not beyond what He has revealed through His Word. A word of caution: in order to be frank, my language may not always be palatable and politically correct. I don't intend to be insulting yet am deliberately refraining from skirting those areas we tend to tiptoe around for fear of insulting someone.

I have written from the realization of my own sinfulness, and of how secularized I had really become, until the Lord started a retransforming work in my own life over the last few years. It is with that imperfect self that I invite you to join me on this journey.

Some views expressed stem from my interaction with other cultures and religions. Having spent large segments of time in Muslim areas of

Eastern Africa, coming home in between has been a shocking experience. To my eyes, our Western societies have managed to become more immodest at each of my return visits. It also appeared that the majority of Christians did not seem to mind and that a number have happily gone along with the trend. Looking around at the dilapidation of common decency and modesty, I cannot help but wonder whether as Christians we have given up on informing the larger culture. It rather looks as if Christians have been swept along the numbing road to self-actualization and mind anaesthetization.

INTRODUCTION

Idolatry has engulfed us and acculturation has lulled us to sleep. Are we Western Christians ready to stand in Christ in the face of increasing hostility towards Christianity?

W estern culture appears to be pushing the envelope of social boundaries ever further, and the contrast with the Eastern world I served is increasingly stark. Additionally, it looks as though Western Christians have tacitly accepted the predominant culture's progression into hedonism and social adulation, and seem quite unfazed at such progression. On one hand, diversity is admired, and so it should; at the same time increasingly bizarre lifestyles are applauded and normalized, even legalized. On the other hand, it appears to be quite acceptable to ridicule and demonize any Christian who takes a stand for what he or she believes. I am not speaking of the strident, confrontational, and often embarrassing outspokenness of some, but of those who with quiet strength resist the erosion of values that has insinuated every layer of our society. *Christophobia* has become an accepted behaviour.

How did we get to this point, and how can we Christians raise ourselves back out of these traps and regain our saltiness? In the following chapters we shall examine some of the culprits, traps, and idols that beset us, and contemplate a move forward in holistic ways that honour and exalt God. We shall look at the path of our downward slide, to the present state of affairs. Next we shall explore how to reclaim and redeem ourselves and those things we use on a daily basis. Finally, we shall see how we can become ready to withstand the increasing hostility that we already are, and will be facing as Western Christians.

We shall look at both the positive and negative influences that multiculturalism has in Christians' lives.

Believers from the Global South (Asia, Africa, Latin America) have generously shared their faith stories within a Western narrative. Their stories are found throughout, at the end of some chapters. Some of the names have been changed, to protect the identity of the individuals.

As I wrote and pondered on God's kingdom, I was, and still am, overwhelmed by God's unconditional love, and at the same time weighed down with our indifference to this God we claim to love and serve. Our gospel of salvation, without the outworking of our faith that embodies Jesus' Sermon on the Mount, has become an empty gospel. Yes, it is wonderful when the lost find their way to Jesus, and it is vital to find eternal life in Him, but then what? How do new believers live out this salvation? How does it translate into daily Western life in such a way that it transforms the communities we live in, the friends we socialize with, the colleagues we work with, and the families we share life with? How should we look forward to Christ's coming again, which, in our postmodern era, seems more and more like a fairy tale? The proclamation of the gospel cannot stay at the spoken stage. The cheapening of the gospel by words that don't demonstrate congruence with our actions is not very convincing. Is it surprising, then, that not more people come to faith in Christ? Too often believers feel that once they have shared the gospel and their testimony, the job is done, sounding a bit like: "Get with the program, turn your life around, and join me in church . . . if not, well, don't waste my time; there are more souls to save."

This may sound shocking to some readers, yet Western Christianity has shown no teeth. While many truly desire the spiritual salvation of those still separated from Christ, the cost of getting involved in those people's lives is for most of us too high a price to pay. Befriending those outside our household of faith, for the sheer purpose of loving and respecting all of God's human beings, is too emotionally taxing (beyond our structured Sunday and Bible study and other church setting/program). Our reaching out therefore remains at a utilitarian level. If there is no quick acceptance of the gospel, let's move on to the next soul; I am speaking as someone who has been down this road.

Jesus never modelled this kind of thoughtless relating; and, though it be well-intentioned, production-line evangelism outreach cannot produce profound and lasting fruit. It may be quick and dirty for those who want to "do outreach," and may provide a feel-good sensation, but reaching out is anything but quick and dirty. Imagine God listening to our petitions, nodding absent-mindedly, and indifferently moving on to the next petitioner. I believe if He were to treat us in such way, we would feel deeply rejected, insignificant, and hurt, even offended. Maybe it goes much deeper than that; maybe our utilitarian and effortless approach stands in direct proportion to how *we* relate to God. Let's find out how this may have happened unawares and look at ways to change direction.

By the end of *Hijacked! Idols in Disguise*, as fellow pilgrims we may have been encouraged in holding firm to, and living out biblical values in the face of opposition; we may feel challenged from inertia to action; hopefully I will have achieved a small contribution to the heralding of the kingdom of God and our cooperating with it. I wish courage and much joy in our journey together to rediscovering a greater closeness to God and defeating the idols that distract us.

CHAPTER 1

Recognizing the Idols
That Seduce Us

[Idols] ... are lifeless producers of death, part of the created world, controlling and dominating, binding humans into chains of necessity, and—being unable to speak—they work to enslave by means of the visual.—Andrew Goddard (*False Producers in the Bible*)

It may be quite depressing to investigate the many idols the Enemy uses to entice Christians into distraction. But let's take heart; there is hope and freedom from the bonds of idolatry. It takes a diagnosis of our spiritual health before we can deal with the disease and be healed.

Consider this: during a dinner with friends and fellow seminary graduates, a question arose. According to Acts 15, "The Jerusalem council instructed Gentile believers to 'abstain from things polluted by idols, from fornication, from whatever had been strangled and from blood.'" What does "abstain from things polluted by idols" mean for us today?" Most around the table agreed that it was a personal matter and different for every Christian. None, however, was willing to specify what those idols could be. The reactions seem to underline an unease and reluctance to define something that might require us to question our lifestyles, let alone change them. If we don't name our idols, they remain unseen and harmless, or so we think. The issue becomes vital for Christians who grapple with defining where secular culture ends and Christianity begins in a largely acculturated

Western faith. It is a challenge for young people, in particular, to discern godly voices from the siren's song. In *The Grand Inquisitor Lives,* Alonzo McDonald suggests, "False gods that are more devious and difficult to deal with are factors that are basically good most of the time. They become idols only when they are misused and pursued to excess."[1]

Good things can become idols, indeed; have we been captivated unawares?

An idol, according to Richard Keyes,

> is something within creation that is inflated to function as a substitute for God. . . . Idolatry may not involve explicit denials of God's existence of character. It may well come in the form of an overattachment to something that is, in itself, perfectly good. The crucial warning is this: As soon as our loyalty to anything leads us to disobey God, we are in danger of making it an idol.[2]

Keyes explains, for instance, how work, which is ordained by God, can become an idol if pursued to the exclusion of relational family responsibilities. On the other hand, family elevated above all other relationships and obligations is also a form of idolatry. "Idols will inevitably involve self-centeredness, self-inflation and self-deception [by] counterfeiting God."[3]

As Christians we have the tendency to see our church community as pure, and other Christian denominations as being too secular. We are quick to assign guilt to Christian circles that do not adhere to the standards we hold. The same goes for idolatry. We seldom see this as a problem in our own circles but can define them quite easily for other religions, liberal churches, and the unchurched. We are inclined to forget that the Bible warns us of the deceitfulness of our hearts (Jeremiah 17:9) and is, as Os Guinness states, "the supreme idol-making factory" that too readily buys into modern technology, rides along the wave of consumerism and partakes in contemporary hedonism.[4]

Regardless of our place in history, it is human nature to rationalize our cultural values and norms within our epoch. And because of that we often fail to see those pernicious rationalizations that go against God. Anyone who speaks out against the trends of the day is called intolerant, Luddite, backwards, and so on. When those rationalizations are threatened, defenses go up, and the instinct is to plug our ears and loudly object.

As Christians we are not immune to our own rationalizations when we try to justify being different while cloaking our worldliness in a Christian mantle. Music is a case in point.

From households of faith, to denominations, to radio and television, to music and books—any may unwittingly become an idol. This is not to suggest that we should not partake of Christian content; not at all. We nonetheless need to be aware that in our desire for Christian-focused content, we have failed to recognize that we have merely created a parallel world. A world, for instance, where we transpose music from popular culture into a Christian stream by simply adding Christian-like lyrics to the same music, making it acceptable to a Christian audience. As it is, most music that is hailed as "Christian" does not in fact make it so. Music should rest on its own merit. A Christian artist who composes out of reverence for his or her God-given gift will compose from that depth. His or her work will be original; it will be theologically sound and will praise the Creator, not the creature.

Ironically, most companies that now promote a "Christian" line of music and publish a "Christian" line of fiction are secular agencies, such as Time-Warner and Harlequin. Secular companies have discovered there is much profit to be made from an exploding Christian market. But it is safe to assume that ensuing profits do not necessarily support Christian endeavours. These companies are not interested in how music and books affect the audience, or in whether the contents are sound. This we need to guard against at all cost.

It is natural, of course, to long for Christian relationships where we can feel at home, speak the same language, and form safe friendships, without having to interact with those who do not share the same values. It is this insular environment that masks itself as a subculture. At the same time, remaining in our subculture robs the outsider from a loving concern and dialogue that can inform a different lifestyle and bring about a transformation. Meeting with like-minded Christians, with our tribe, so to speak, we no longer feel the need to reach outside our Christian community, and this is not what we are called to do. Paul tells us that we are to live in the world and yet not be part of it, and Jesus asks of His

Father: "My prayer is not that you take them out of the world but that you protect them from the Evil One. They are not of the world, even as I am not of it" (John 17:15–16, NIV). We can count on God for daily protection from evil while we live in this world and pray that we not be tempted by its values, which would alienate us from God.

Dietrich Bonhoeffer said,

> I discovered . . . that it is only by living completely in this world that one learns to have faith. By this-worldliness I mean living unreservedly in life's duties, problems, successes, failures. In so doing we throw ourselves completely into the arms of God, taking seriously not our own suffering but those of God in the world.[5]

Bonhoeffer believed that real faith was evident by our living fully and doing our work and activities in the presence of God, which included caring for those outside the household of faith. It means to living very much in this world without being part of its humanistic philosophies, instead inoculating it with Christ's life-giving values.

The Power and Influence of the Secular World around Us

In order to infuse the world around us with Christ's values, we need to be aware of its idolatrous power on us. Living with the tension of "living in the world" and "without being part of it" requires wisdom.

As Christians we are prone to compartmentalize the secular and the sacred. Each era we live in tends to colour our worldview, and as Christians we can't entirely escape the influence the dominant culture has on our daily living.

It is therefore significant to observe the daily incongruity of how we exercise our faith in a secular environment, be it work or leisure, and how we tend to contradict that belief in our actions. Many of us don't notice, for instance, the dichotomy of proclaiming dependence on God for our daily needs while on the other hand working too hard at earning a living and accumulating material possessions inconsistent with New Testament models. We need to protect ourselves from a false sense of security in our belief and be very aware to what extent the secular influences us.

In several gospel passages we are warned against anyone who "preaches another gospel." Os Guinness notes the popularity of "two bogus beatitudes—health and happiness."[6] Just like children, we run after the pied pipers who sell us those "bogus beatitudes," which come to us through television advertising and other media. Even some of our churches, where pagan notions have come to intermingle with orthodoxy, blind us to the dangerous consequences of this mix. In 1984 Bob Goudzwaard stated,

> In their pursuit of prosperity, salvation, health, protection and so forth, people sooner or later create gods. But gods never leave their makers alone. . . . It is conceivable then that the means to progress which our own hands have made—the economy, technology, science and the state—have become such forces today, imposing their will on us as gods. … How can we expect national conversion if we Christians do not admit that we too are accomplices in the basic wrongs of our country and of the world?[7]

It is essential therefore that we recognize the secular idolatrous forces that press upon us from all sides, in order to resist them. Not paying attention to their lure will inevitably consume us. It is much harder to step out of the trap once we have taken the bait than if we had avoided it in the first place. God's grace, in Jesus, reaches out to help us remove the trap if we find ourselves incapable of escape. We can count on it!

To find out if something is idolatrous, we must look at the things in our lives that consume us. It will be up to us individually to sift through our daily activities and replace with godly values anything that has become, or is on its way to becoming, idolatrous.

Questions
1. What pursuits have been captivating my imagination and may have pushed aside my relationship with God and with those I love?
2. What activities have become consuming to the point of my neglecting more important issues?

3. Have family members or friends voiced their concern that I'm spending too much time [fill in what applies to you, e.g., online, in front of the TV, playing computer games, etc.].

Prayer

God, with your grace, grant me the strength to acknowledge what has taken priority above all else. Open my eyes and my heart to admit where I have become enslaved, so that You can bring forgiveness and healing in those areas of my life.

CHAPTER TWO

Generations in Motion

Each generation imagines itself to be more intelligent than the one that went before it, and wiser than the one that comes after it.—George Orwell

In each successive generation there exists an innate tension to change the status quo of the older generation and to discard those values and mores that hamper personal expression and too obediently follow societal conventions. Each generation tends to look down at the previous generation and then turns around and disapproves of the changes the next one brings about. Such attitudes have existed since the dawn of humanity and will continue. For our purpose, let's take a bird's-eye view of the generations we find ourselves with:

1. The baby boomers, born between 1946 and 1964;
2. Generation X, also called the latchkey generation, born between 1965 and 1976;
3. Generation Y, born between 1977 and 1983;
4. Generation Z, born after 1983.

For the baby boomers, taking hold of sexual freedoms, celebrating individualism, and consequently rebelling against the perceived stifling conventional customs of the time were the hallmarks of their generation, embodied by the hippie movement.

For the Western Christian it was still an era in which faith was worn as a badge of pride and a symbol of a wholesome lifestyle, marked by respect for church authority and for the law of the land. This was a period when young adults entering the workforce had no problem finding work. The economy was booming, employment was thriving, the sky was the limit, and life was good; that is, people could afford to buy modern appliances and other material goods that provided a pleasant lifestyle. People worked hard, without questioning authority, but also reaped the benefits of their labour, which in turn assured a better life than those of their parents and grandparents, who experienced the Great Depression of the thirties and suffered, to a greater or lesser extent, through two World Wars.

The baby boomer generation saw the beginning and peak of the hippie movement. When school dress codes no longer had to be rigorously adhered to, young people started to let their hair grow long. Young men grew long beards. Young women wore long, colourful dresses, and young men wore caftans over casual, often colourful, pants. Hippies embraced peace, evidenced by the loud protests during the Vietnam War. Hippies became associated with drugs, free love, communes, and raucous music. Many baby boomers of the sixties and seventies acknowledge having been part of the hippie movement or at its fringes.

Generation X is a generation marked by lower birth rates and rising divorce rates. Work was seen as a means to provide a lifestyle rather than something to be pursued for its own rewards. Gen X-ers like to research and learn on their own, taking full advantage of what technology has to offer to achieve results. They are natural problem solvers who thrive on doing things as long as there is a direct benefit for them. They appreciate feedback that is relevant and take action accordingly.

Critical of the baby boomers, Gen X-ers see the previous generation as one who squandered natural resources and left the next generation to pick up the pieces of an eroded environment. They also criticize the baby boomers for causing the downward shift in economic opportunities. Gen X-ers started experiencing how university degrees no longer provided guaranteed career tracks.

Political correctness enters the stage.

Generation Y is the more impatient of the four generations. Gen Y-ers have a shorter attention span, and their minds need to be constantly challenged to new ideas and actions. Gen Y-ers pride themselves for being multitaskers, being adept at, for instance, grasping what others say in a conversation while surfing the Internet and replying to a telephone call. They enjoy teamwork and collective projects, and have embraced technology to the point where they need to be in touch 24/7. Because technology has increased the speed of delivery of information and acquisition of goods and entertainment, they have become used to and expect instant gratification and rewards.

Most Generation Y-ers have grown up with both parents pursuing careers. Left largely unattended and without a parent to guide them through acceptable societal boundaries and responsibilities, Gen Y-ers saw the onset of an entitled and self-absorbed generation. Peers, media, and Internet inform their actions and thought.

Christian Gen Y-ers find increasing difficulties in navigating faith in everyday life. With an entertainment-based larger society, they find their parents' faith expressions and places of worship irrelevant. A large number of Christian churches have shifted to a more entertainment-focused worship and preaching in theatre-like church buildings. Health and prosperity movements that had started during Generation X have garnered a greater following through media and the Internet. Generation Y Christians want to hear a pain-free, feel-good gospel.

Political correctness is in full bloom.

Generation Z has experienced the full explosion of mobile technology. Gen Z-ers are not only comfortable with this technology but are fully at home with it, leaving the other generations to grapple with the rapid technological changes. Gen Z-ers adapt and learn quickly and thrive on the next new breakthrough in technology. Social media is their preferred mode of interaction and is embraced as standard communication. They tend to be loners, are more self-absorbed, and do not easily engage in teamwork or personal social interaction. Because everything seems to be at their beck and call, instant gratification is the norm, and probably at a heightened degree compared to their predecessors. Gen Z-ers cannot imagine life without being connected every second of the day.

Generation Z is a generation of both entitlement and despair. Because of the environmental and economical messes left by the previous generations, Gen Z-ers feel strongest about society owing them a living.

Working parents, who at the end of the day have little time left for their children, try to assuage their guilt by indulging their children. This further increases the sense of entitlement by their children.

Reality shows and entertainment have become models for how to live life. Educated youth cannot find meaningful work in their professions of choice. A few bright stars make it big, particularly in the world of social media, which provides large financial returns but few real job opportunities for the masses.

Christian Gen Z-ers are caught in the same maelstrom as the predominant society and are not immune to media and entertainment influences. With most Christian families where both parents work, these children too find Christian faith irrelevant. Church attendance (in the West) is at an all-time low. Fewer people give to the church, either financially or of their time. Christian Gen Z-ers are exposed to the same self-absorption and self-directed living as their secular peers.

Political correctness has reached absurd proportions and is fully entrenched in society.

It is of course nothing new that with each successive generation, a shift away from earlier values and sense of propriety takes place. Whether this shift is deliberate or simply sliding into new conventions may depend on one's relationships to older generations and authority figures. These shifts do not necessarily mean they are wrong; they may simply mirror the relentless changes that each generation undergoes through the ages. To resist change is not always helpful. On the other hand, to accept every wind of change can be problematic, especially if it moves a culture towards a destructive trend without a corrective factor along the way. Self-absorbed individualism and celebrated ego-directed lifestyles are ultimately unfulfilling and leave one open to espousing philosophies that may promise meaning without, in the end, delivering on the promise.

The implication of technological advances would suggest that most of the Millennials are progressively losing their social skills. Text messaging, Facebook, and Twitter, among others, are replacing valuable face-to-face time. Verbal and, in particular, nonverbal cues observed in person are missed, and the art of communication is adversely affected. "[U]nreflective use of communications technology will make life 'increasingly empty as entire populations become unable to discern what is valuable from what is valueless, replacing wisdom with trivial information.'"[8]

This triviality manifests itself best through the dawn of celebrity worship, as online communities feverishly tweet every sneeze of their stars. The garish and the immoral have replaced thoughtful art as a gift to be shared with humanity. Scandals fill the online tabloids and fill the recipients' minds with hollow pictures and thoughts, numbing them to the insidious lies that these "heroes'" lives represent.

However, according to Pew Internet Research, interesting findings are contradicting those who believe that social media and the Internet are creating more isolation and less personal contact. In its 2009 survey, there was an astonishing growth in personal contact and interaction due to the use of social media. An individual's circle of influence has increased, and people using social media, text messaging, and mobile telephones have greater contact with their neighbourhood, volunteer circles, and community. The research does not indicate whether these ways of relating are more intimate or meaningful, although some of the responses to the Pew survey seem to indicate that they provided an immediate network of support in a time of crisis.[9]

A 2011 survey on the future of Millennials in 2020, looked even more promising,[10] although a number of non-randomly chosen participants voiced concerns at the negative impact of the rapid-fire communications, by warning that information gathering will become superficial, and that people will be able to digest only sound bites. Those who responded favourably commented that in the future minds would continue to change and adapt and would have the ability to process and synthesize information quickly. At the same time, we need to be aware that the ongoing torrents of information, and the ability to access information on the spot, has diminished our capacity to remember what we have read, seen, and heard. Nevertheless, Millennials in general will be able to fashion large and wide-ranging social networks and harness global connections at an unprecedented speed. As Christians who participate in these technologies, we are in an exceptional position to redeem the aspect of meaningful electronic and personal interactions these networks represent.

From the various studies it appears that, when channelled properly, technology and social media can enrich lives by eliminating geographical boundaries, thus bringing diverse cultures closer together. Striking the right balance between virtual and personal interactions is a crucial element by which our attitudes toward family, neighbour, and stranger can glorify God.

Uninhibited acceptance and use of technology, social media, and all other activities that consume the daily lives of Christians will, by and large, continue to blind them to the subtle erosion of biblical values and priorities. Many of the secular values promoted through computer games, educational television programs, entertainment, and leisure activities are contrary to kingdom values. Maybe parents and Christians in general feel that as long as they protect their children from these influences and remain in their own Christian enclaves, the worst exposure to potentially harmful games, entertainment, and such will be avoided. Unfortunately, the reality is that children are exposed to secular values while they explore the world "out there," in the world of education, in entertainment, or when staying over at friends homes and away from parental supervision.

All of this has led us to place great value on our careers, homes, money, power, and children. In turn, these become our idols because of the time and energy we focus on them. Reversing this trend requires a willingness to examine some of the idols that have tiptoed into our lives. We will reflect on a few; some may even come as a surprise.

Questions
1. Which of the generations do I belong to or do I identify with most closely?
2. How many of my generation's values have I adopted?
3. Of those, how many can I consider in harmony with Scriptures, as counterscriptural, or as acceptable although strictly secular? (I may have to consult Scripture passages to determine whether some of the values I take for granted might be contradicting God's values.)

Prayer
God, by your grace help me to identify where I stand in my daily life and what values I need to re-evaluate.
[Take time to prayerfully make a list of those things the Holy Spirit brings to mind.]

CHAPTER 3

Pluralism

There is neither Jew nor Gentile, neither slave nor free, nor is there male and female, for you are all one in Christ Jesus.—
Galatians 3:28, NIV

I n today's reality, multiculturalism and pluralism occupy increasing space in our societies. They affect how we treat one another. The changing multicultural demographics compels Christians to take notice; other cultures, religions, and philosophies demand to be heard.

This reality has caused a shift in policy making, governance, and the way religious circles have in part succumbed to the pressure of accommodating and complying with a politically correct environment. On the other hand, a pluralistic society, where Christianity is no longer the dominant religion, offers fertile opportunities for evangelism: the mission field has come to us. How, then, are we influencing those of other faiths and philosophies? Do our lifestyles and pursuits demonstrate kingdom values? Can others see Christ's love manifest in our actions and attitudes? How are we, as Western Christians, viewed by those cultures who now surround us and have become as much a part of our national fabric as we have?

Many Western Christians have been lamenting the loss of the Lord's Prayer and Christian symbols in public schools and institutions. It may be understandable that they feel protective of these sacred symbols, as Canada and the United States were founded on Judeo-Christian values, which historically permeated all areas of public life. We need to accept that over the last thirty years, Western countries have seen a tremendous influx of immigrants from cultural and religious backgrounds that do not espouse our symbols. Immigrants from Mexico and Central and South America may readily acknowledge Christian practices and symbols, since they are common in their countries of origin. On the other hand, today many more people hail from countries with differing faiths and philosophies. Newcomers are discovering freedom of expression in our democratic countries, along with the right to freely practise their philosophies or beliefs. This freedom entails public display of their own religious symbols without having to suffer persecution for doing so.

Although both practicing and nominal Western Christians are statistically still in the majority, freedom offered by democracy inherently respects the rights of all. We can no longer claim to be the dominant voice for virtue and principles. Freedom is a double-edged sword that comes with good and evil, moral and immoral values. For Christians, biblical values and beliefs are the only truth. We are under obligation to honour, respect, and love our neighbour and to show the same concern God has for each person regardless of race, religion, or philosophy. This entails acceptance of all faith symbols worn by respective groups. By no means is this an abdication of our Christian values and convictions; on the contrary, it opens the way to meaningful dialogue and exchange of ideas. It is our duty to listen attentively to the other while standing firm in our own belief. If anything, we as Christians need to keep our governments accountable and should speak up when equal rights, such as freedom of expression, are violated. We should question and challenge practices, such as those found in politically correct language, that border the absurd. Holding fast or challenging areas of civic life that affect the rights of Christians does not absolve us from demonstrating kingdom values. The injunction "Do not conform any longer to the pattern of this world" (Rom. 12:2, NIV) is closely followed by "If it is possible, so far as it depends on you, live peaceably with all" (Rom 12:18, ESV). These two commands go hand in hand, and resisting those things in the world that go against God must be accompanied by living in peace with everyone while forgoing obnoxious, belligerent, or self-righteous speech and attitudes. It may well be that negative criticisms or comments made by our Christian culture are based on fear—fear of how the "others" may impose "their" values or beliefs and infringe upon "our" way of life.

Feeling threatened invariably engenders subconscious intolerance, which may translate into open or passive aggressive behaviour or language that may further alienate people from Christianity. For example, a study referenced in a mainstream American newspaper found that the majority of Americans are circumspect in their attitudes towards Muslims.[11] Muslims, on the other hand, felt that their leaders had contributed to these attitudes by not taking a strong stance against extremist Muslims.

A Pew Research Center study states:

> Many Muslims fault their own leaders for failing to challenge Islamic extremists. Nearly half (48%) say that Muslim leaders in the United States have not done enough to speak out against Islamic extremists; only about a third (34%) say Muslim leaders have done enough in challenging extremists. At the same time, 68% say that Muslim Americans themselves are cooperating as much as they should with law enforcement. … For Muslims in the United States, concerns about Islamic extremism coexist with the view that life for Muslim Americans in post-9/11 America is difficult in a number of ways. Significant numbers report being looked at with suspicion (28%), and being called offensive names (22%). And while 21% report being singled out by airport security, 13% say they have been singled out by other law enforcement. Overall, a 52% majority says that government anti-terrorism policies single out Muslims in the U.S. for increased surveillance and monitoring.[12]

The misdeeds of a few are visited on an entire cultural or religious group. The experience of Muslims in America is not unique or exclusive to them; we can find similar experiences among the First Nations in Canada or Roma in Europe, where general attitudes towards their beliefs or traditions are still viewed by many with some animosity or hostility.

In other words, it is a global phenomenon that shows how easy it is to be prejudiced when we feel threatened.

Present global changes have facilitated pluralism. Not all of it has been positive. Whether a country's immigration allows for rapid integration depends on the policies in place that promote integration. In Canada, for instance, integration is not required per se; people from different cultures can live in their enclaves without having to adjust to a Canadian way of life. Called a cultural mosaic, this too became an idol in its own right. For the sake of accepting and accommodating, the Canadian government has bent over backwards to adjust to the many different cultures, rather than the other way around. As a Chinese friend put it, "You can live in Canada as a Chinese, without having to change anything." It may sound wonderful, but what it does is fragment citizens within a country. There are entire neighbourhoods with shops, professional services, and so on where people speak their own language. That in itself is not new; what is new is that if, as an English-speaking Canadian, you walk into one of these shops, the owners or attendants can't even address you in English.

The consequence is a divided society where, for the sake of tolerance—another modern idol (political correctness when taken to the extreme, for instance)—civil servants pretzel themselves to fit and accept demands and rights of every cultural group. A country so pressured to comply to the whim of its pluralistic society becomes weak and loses its identity.

Yet it is an incredible privilege to live in a pluralistic society. It represents a microcosm of what the kingdom of God is all about. God in Christ redeems and calls people of every nation and ethnicity. This call is a vivid reminder of God's creativity and all-encompassing love across all ethnic groups. Every day brings new opportunities to welcome cultures we interact with into the kingdom of God, by showing love and respect and by the way we live out our faith.

On the downside, a pluralistic society can tempt Christians into isolation and ethnocentricity; this can happen by associating in Christian subcultures with mostly Christian friends, music, books, church programs, and other Christian activities. It cuts us off from what we were called to be as ambassadors of Christ. There is a real danger in spending time exclusively in Christian pursuits; believers come to a place where making friends with those who do not belong to the household of faith feels uncomfortable instead of engaging, and so avoid forming meaningful relationships with non-Christians. We thus fail to see that when we keep our everyday activities at work or school separate from our Christian pursuits, we rob non-Christian colleagues or fellow students from witnessing God's grace, love, and care in our lives.

On the flip side of this menace is the snare of getting too wrapped up in multiculturalism and social good, to the point of forgetting that all of us Christians are in need of the redemptive infusion of Christ and of the Holy Spirit. Touting pluralism may lead to a slippery slope of turning it into an idol.

In all circumstances, we need to be vigilant and put our absolute trust in God's work and ask Christ to show us how to conduct ourselves in a pluralistic society in a way that speaks and breathes His kingdom. We must be living testimonies of God's power to love, forgive, and unify nations to Him. Such can only happen when we fully understand our identity as citizens of a nation and kingdom that is eternal while living in the tension of the here and now.

Questions

1. Where have I been sidetracked from living out my faith in everyday life, living a religious life?
2. Is my Christian walk consistent from Sunday to Saturday or am I content with being a Sunday and mid-week Christian?
3. Do I give in to exaggerated forms of political correctness for fear of being ridiculed as a Christian?
4. Is the way I lead my life as a follower of Christ relevant and thought-provoking to outsiders? Or do I need to reassess and ask God to bring changes?
5. Where, when, and how has my daily life shown disregard or a self-righteous attititude to those who belong to a different tradition and belief system?
6. Do my choices (career, work, entertainment, leisure, home, social environment, etc.) demonstrate intentionality and respect for God and my neighbour? Do they honour God even in secret?

Prayer

God, with your grace, grant me the strength to acknowledge attitudes that are contrary to your will and do not honour you. Forgive me for having been harsh or judgemental toward my neighbor, who may differ from me in culture and beliefs. Open my eyes and awaken my heart to your love, that I may actively love and respect my neighbor as Jesus instructed us. Renew in me a willing spirit and a desire to live out my faith in all aspects of daily life.

CHAPTER 4

Taking into Account Other Views

All community which is founded merely on uniformity of opinion and ways of procedure, without a change of heart, constitutes a harmful sect.—Count Nikolaus Ludwig von Zinzendorf (1700–1760)

The Internet has afforded accessability to most religions and philosophies, enticing people's attention outside of Judeo-Christian values. To elaborate would require a different book altogether; hence, the following is meant to give us a snapshot of what is out there, to serve as a sense of what distractions, imitations and conterfeit values we face.

On the increase is the acceptance of manifold philosophies anchored in paganism, humanism and atheism. In one sense this is nothing new. These doctrines have always existed, although many of them used to be practiced within secret societies, and some still are. What is different now is that with the dawn of online chat rooms and websites, these societies have become more visible and accessible. The web allows people disenchanted with traditional religion, or prevalent world systems, to seek out alternatives and connect with New Age movements and other groups that fit their version of religion.

Too many Christian institutions have lost their relevance and have failed to bring solace or tangible care to hurting people. Consequently, people withdraw or, in desperation, go online to seek answers in the most unlikely places. Once they find a sounding board or someone who can seemingly bring them hope, they become more deeply entrenched in worlds such as the occult.

Often the increase in popularity of the occult can be attributed to celebrities or socialites who enthusiastically endorse a given pagan belief. In turn, their fan base check out what is special about their idols' beliefs. What may have started out as mere curiosity ends up becoming their philosophy too, maybe even mixed with the faith they grew up with, thus taking the bits they like from each doctrine.

The Rise of Pagan Societies

According to a BBC site on religions, paganism encompasses diverse communities, with some groups concentrating on specific traditions, practices or elements, such as Wiccans, Druids, shamans, sacred ecologists, and Odinists.[13] With access to the Internet, interest in these pagan communities has grown and continues to gain momentum. These occult traditions have become more acceptable under the larger New Age umbrella, where Eastern religions, paganism, and Christianity are joined in syncretic fashion.

Wicca has become more prevalent, and as Christians we need to be aware of its presence and its attraction, which existed in ancient biblical times; God clearly condemned their practices. Purveyors of magic and divination prey on people's deepest longings and fears, bringing about a desire to know one's fate; a deception that it is very much alive today. As a matter of fact, judging from the proliferation of their TV shows and online offerings, clairvoyants are doing brisk business. For example, in Europe, especially in the Mediterranean countries, there can be as many as five channels airing such programs.

Kabbalah, a mystical teaching that emerged out of Judaism, is in the the spotlight today, thanks to celebrities. The Kabbalah Center in Los Angeles, California, made popular through references by Madonna et al., has contributed to its tremendous growth and interest. In its popularized form, it attracts those seeking mystical or "secret" experiences and magic. Orthodox Jews will disavow the practice of magic, which is condemned in the Torah and which they say was never part of the true Kabbalah.

Kabbalists are quick to point out that Kaballah, while mystical, is not a religion and that it has no semblance to any of the aforementioned groups.

Scientology (the study of knowledge and truth); "a person is not a body but a spirit," according to Scientology, for example, came to the fore through actors such as Tom Cruise and John Travolta.

We should not underestimate the power of celebrity influence that draws more and more followers. This is true of all pagan religions and pseudo-Christian organizations.

Most of these movements have their origins in the occult and demonstrate that Satan is ever at work trying to thwart God's redemptive work by offering a counterfeit, man-centered, idolatrous redemption that ultimately leads to spiritual death and eternal separation from God.

Atheism has also become more visible, newsworthy and "mainstream,"[14] especially thanks to outspoken and well-known people like Professor Richard Dawkins, who, through his books and anti-God position, has had a profound impact on the case for atheism. Atheism comprises the following strains: humanism,[15] secularism,[16] rationalism,[17] postmodernism,[18] and Unitarian Universalism.[19.] These varieties have become so commonplace that they have seeped into our daily existance.

Postmodernism, the present-day trend, looks at the world as being in a state of constant change. There are no absolutes, and followers can borrow art and views from different philosophies, values, and beliefs to justify their own lifestyles. God is not narrowly defined and can be a blend of various faiths, resulting in syncretism: one makes up his or her own understanding of God, and truth becomes relative. This, of course, is very attractive for many and is embraced in much of our Western world. The fact that through syncretism one creates one's own idol is largely lost.

Buddhism was founded in north-eastern India in the fifth century before Christ. It doesn't have a god as creator, and its philosophy aspires to reach nirvana—freedom from suffering. There are two major traditions, Theravada and Mahayana.

Hinduism, mainly practised in South Asia, comprises various philosophies that all have reincarnation in common. Believers worship a collection of gods and goddesses. Best known to Westerners are Shiva, Vishnu, and Kali; Krishna is one of the incarnations of Vishnu. Hinduism has become popular in the West through the New Age movement, yoga, and Eastern meditation.

Islam, founded in the Arabian peninsula in the seventh century, counts more than a billion adherents worldwide. It comprises two major groups, Sunni and Shia. Islam holds to a rigid moral and religious Shari'a law. The Qur'an is their holy book revealed to the prophet Mohammed, who is accepted by Muslims as the last of the prophets. Conservative and fundamentalist Muslims actively seek to recruit followers and convert them to Islam. Because of the billion-plus worldwide adherents, it has become a significant religion in North America.

In Canada, Muslims had more than doubled their numbers in 2001 from the previous decade, according to Statistics Canada, representing 2 percent of the total population.

In the United States:

> In combination with U.S. Census data, Pew Research Center demographers estimate that there were about 1.8 million Muslim adults and 2.75 million Muslims of all ages (including children under age eighteen) living in the United States in 2011. This represents an increase of roughly 300,000 adults and 100,000 Muslim children since 2007. [20]

Between 2001 and 2005, it appears that Muslims in Western European countries made up between 1.5% and 9.6% of the population, Italy having the lowest numbers and France the highest. According to a Pew Research Center figure, there was an increase in the Muslim population of ten million to seventeen million in 2010.[21]

With the influx of people subscribing to non Judeo-Christian traditions, Western countries have felt increasingly under threat, especially from those who belong to Islam.

We need to understand that values, such as respect for others, honouring God, honest work ethics and so on, remain constant across demoninational lines. Traditions however, vary greatly depending on geographical roots, religious upbringing and so forth. These are what tend to alienate, and cause misunderstandings, suspicion and marginalisation towards those who do not think like we Westerners do; African Americans during the Civil Rights movement as a case in point.

So, Where Do We Stand?

It is not uncommon to find Christians who believe in reincarnation and mix Christian beliefs with occult Eastern philosophies present in Hinduism. Because New Age has successfully insinuated itself into Christianity through innocuous and Christian-sounding theories, it is leading a growing number of Christians astray. Yoga, which is based on hatha yoga, an ancient Hindu system of ascetic practices and meditation, is one of the ways this idolatrous practice has infiltrated Christian circles. (The ultimate goal of yoga meditation is to connect with the divine). It is precisely because it has become commonplace and seen as innocuous, healthy exercise that it is so dangerous.

To a lesser extent, strains of the other aforementioned philosophies have insinuated themselves into Christian circles. By pretending to be angels of light, these philosophies lead many Christians astray or induce them to at least include some of these philosophies in their devotions, thus perverting the sacred into the profane. It can be so subtle that it catches one unawares.

Fundamentalist Christian groups are vociferous in indicting occultic and esoteric practices, and rightfully so. Nevertheless, the generally belligerent tone of their message does not endear and so tends to be summarily ignored or dismissed. It does not help that these fundamentalist groups, who have a tendency to throw out the proverbial baby with the bathwater, get labeled as "backwater" Christians or as "those" groups, hence removing any credibility they might otherwise have.

At the same time, by ignoring changing demographics, and multicultural and multifaith transformations in Western countries, Western Christians have lost the influence for good that we possessed until the end of the nineteenth and the early twentieth century. Moreover, by tragically allowing infiltration of philosophies that are far from Christian, Christianity is heading into an ever-growing danger of apostasy.

The stories shared by Christians from the Global South in their own words throughout this book express how Christianity is being perceived by those hailing from non-Western countries. Whether the perceptions might be biased is of little importance; what is significant is how we respond to those who belong to other faiths or convictions. Where do we stand? What do we truly believe? How much of the other religious strains have we unwittingly mixed as part of our predominantly postmodern worldview without realizing their idolatrous and occult background?

Cyberspace Christians

The evangelicals among us have been quick to take advantage of the methods and media of the day and have a prolific online presence. Technology, from a Christian perspective, can indeed be harnessed for the good of others when we give it the right priorities.

There were more than one million online religion websites in operation in 2001 according to Brenda Brasher, assistant professor of religion and philosophy at Mount Union College and Alliance, Ohio. Brasher opines that "cyberspace erodes the basis from which religion contributes to the destructive dynamics of Xenophobia … it lessens potential inter-religious hatred."[22]

Maybe Brasher alludes to scholarly online exchanges, where understanding is fostered and most disagreements are voiced in a civil fashion. Therefore, I cannot totally concur with Brasher when it comes to sites outside academia. From various religious websites, there is proof that the opposite is true. Vitriolic language in the comments sections of many of these religious, pagan, and atheist websites indicates that rather than tolerance, interreligious hatred appears to be on the rise, at least among the online communities. The more strident the opinions and counterarguments, the more they incite hatred towards those outside one's religious or philosophical convictions (in these communities, paganism and atheism promote their views with religious fervour and hostility).

Earlier we saw how online communities cause more fragmentation, entrench individualism, and ultimately estrange us from those who are within arm's reach.

Let's explore opposing Christian perspectives along with groups whose activities are diametrically the reverse of what Christ came to proclaim. Without taking any position on whether these virtual communities are right or wrong, let's have the option of drawing our own conclusions, based on scriptural principles, and at the same time be aware of possible hazards.

Online religious practices sprang out of an innate desire to connect with others who shared similar beliefs and convictions. Christians too search online for those who share the same scriptural beliefs and doctrines. Many Western Christians feel that orthodox teachings are no longer present in their local churches, consider many of these churches apostate, and thus justify leaving the church altogether. As a result, these Christians feel at a loss and scour the web to find likeminded people. With the profusion of online communities, virtual churches and organizations claim to possess the truth, while indicting Christianity as having gone apostate.

How can the seeker discern truth from falsehood among those many convincing voices? Herein lies the danger, and unless one is firmly grounded in sound biblical teachings, it is difficult to detect the poisoned arrow hidden in between true statements. Naturally, Christians in favour of virtual Christian communities will counter that by chatting with others who share their views, they can ascertain whether a preacher, a teacher or an apologist is telling the truth. Unfortunately, many start from a skewed premise and have difficulty hearing or accepting those who give cautionary advice or who admonish to seek further clarification and wisdom of those who may not be part of the same group.

Christians throughout the global body of Christ who seek meaningful expressions of their faith or are hungry for fellowship they don't seem to find in their area turn to the Internet to fill a spiritual void and need, to strengthen their faith and break the isolation they would otherwise experience. The drawback may be the danger of falling into heretical teachings and idolatrous dogmas if the leader or pastor the seeker follows subtly deviates from sound doctrine, without necessarily ill intent on the part of the leader. Virtual groups are at risk of becoming sectarian in their conviction that only they possess the truth; this, however, is not inherent to the Internet. There is enough documented evidence of sectarian and closed groups in physical churches or circles. Maybe the risk is greater online, as the adherents may be more susceptible than if they were part of a local church, even when this hazard is not exclusive to online communities. Perhaps people who are disenchanted with the church or who may be more impressionable might unquestioningly accept all of their web pastor's or leader's suggestions and teachings. By and large, being separated from the larger body of Christ, whether online or in person, carries the intrinsic danger of sectarianism and idolatry that Christians participating in online communities need to be aware of and guard against.

One thing is certain; virtual communities of faith will continue to grow and reach out where the traditional local church or assembly are failing their sheep.

Questions

1. Am I quick to impose my Christian views, insist on being right, and judge those who don't believe what I believe?

2. Do I take the time to hear and respect the views of others before requesting equal time? Or do I go immediately on a verbal or written attack?

3. Am I willing to love those who belong to the "enemy' camp for the sake of God's kingdom and entreat God for His mercy?

4. Have I been dabbling in esoteric or occult practices online, thinking them to be harmless? (I may need to write down which ones I have visited or contributed to.)

5. If I'm part of an online church community, how am I involved in meaningful ways that impact others and bring them closer to God?

6. Do I find myself disconnecting from a local church community to seek the safety of a more anonymous online church community?

Prayer

God grant me the courage to face where I have avoided the community of other Christians in my neighbourhood and why. Heavenly Father, if my local church is not heretical, would you grant me the grace to humble myself and accept that even in a broken, imperfect church, you are there for your children, and that I have a responsibility to love my brothers and sisters?

If I dabbled with, or accepted esoteric philosophies, Lord, I repent and renounce them, and by your grace, I shall be able to return to your Word.

Lord, if I have condemned or judged those who belong to faiths and philosophies opposed to my own, forgive me for judging them and grant that I may love them with Your love and that I may remember them in prayer. Remind me, whenever I feel drawn into a heated argument on faith, that Jesus came to save and not condemn sinners. You are the only one who can turn hearts to You.

Gopi's Journey from Hinduism to Christianity

I grew up in a Hindu family; we had our own family temple and were steeped in the faith. On my mother's side, in order to please the gods, the priest would do rituals called *pooja* [Sanskrit]. My parents instructed me in all aspects of the faith. For instance, if I wanted to succeed in my tests, I would pray for ten days and fast for another seven; then success was guaranteed. If I did not fast and pray, then I would fail. My father used to go to the temple every Thursday morning and made an offering of oil lamps in lime shells, placing them all around the temple.

The smell of incense would pervade our house; such was pleasing to the gods. Daily my parents walked with the sticks around the house, and I can still smell the soothing scents of these offerings. I cannot forget my mom's mantras, which she would say every evening around 6:30 p.m., and she would recite them for about half an hour at the top of her lungs while sitting in a yoga position in front of the idol. Even I was very steeped in the Hindu religion and would travel by myself a great distance to reach other temples, sometimes a few thousand kilometres away. I believed a particular temple had the truth because I used to like this one goddess who was my favourite.

In Hinduism there are more than one thousand idols, and one can choose one's favourites.

In February of 2007 I reached Singapore, where I went for my studies. I didn't pray, since I was alone and free, with nobody watching me. I wore a pendant around my neck with my favourite goddess. Whenever I felt worried I'd hold on to the pendant and pray. But I felt a lot of emptiness, and I wasn't sure I would be okay, because I wasn't really sure that I was going in the right direction of life while I was in Singapore.

Around May/June 2007, through some of my close friends, I happened to go to a church one Sunday, which had 2,500 members. I found this church very interesting, because they had vibrant rock bands and nice music with dancing. The pastor had a good sense of humour, and that made me more interested in this church. I started going every Sunday just to listen to the pleasant music and to the pastor's good humour. As time went on I started to think about what the pastor had been preaching about. I got my first Bible, and some verses, such as John 3:16, Psalm 23, were becoming very favourite and personal to me. In the midst of the tensions, these verses would bring some kind of comfort. At some point, while reading the Bible and making baby steps in prayer, I removed my pendant but still kept it, because my parents would certainly ask me about it whenever we'd have a webcam conversation.

Within the church, a small group of people would welcome newcomers and welcome them to the church family. I would be asked about my walk and what problems I'd been going through. For the first time someone asked me to make Jesus my Saviour. Shortly afterwards I met different groups of friends with whom I connected, among whom was my wife—but of course I didn't know that yet. This group of friends started encouraging me to pray, and I tried to do so. I no longer had to travel huge distances to have God with me. This was the biggest truth: that the Lord is with you always. One thing I noticed as a Hindu, whose gods had many arms and weapons, was that this new God, Jesus, had His arms open to welcome me.

In the beginning Jesus only represented another additional god; my journey to faith took different stages before I could see the difference. My biggest support in my Christian growth was my wife, who then was a dearest friend. She told me what it was to be a born again Christian, after which I started to pray when I was alone; I would speak wondering to whom I was speaking, but I would get a sense that I was being heard. Then I learned about the Holy Spirit, and I experienced His infilling, which brought me to the next level of my Christian growth and awareness.

Shortly afterwards I had a feeling that I should work for the church. I became worried, because I wasn't baptized or a Christian, I was only a very new believer, and would they accept me? One of the Sundays, a brother in Christ told me about different opportunities available in the church and asked me to fill in an application; he was unaware of my misgivings to work in the church. The next day I received a call to serve in the church in the position of receiving new believers. They called me for an interview, asked me a few questions about what I believed, and asked me to join the very next week. I was very excited and scared at the same time. I, who was born into a Hindu family, was now working in a Christian church. If my parents found out about it, they would kill me! So when I was alone, the

Holy Spirit spoke to me: "When you believe in Christ, why do you worry so much about your parents? After your death you will be sure to be in heaven, but your parents will not be there with you, and they will ask you: 'Why didn't you tell us?'" So I decided to speak to my mother about my new beliefs. I started telling her in a simple way, and she was okay with it but didn't tell my dad. She said she used to go to a Catholic church when she was younger. At that time I didn't have enough guts to say more and decided I would tell them more at a later date.

I started serving in the welcome centre and found out that there were people who weren't believers who would come to the church. Then I could really see the difference between them and real believers, although I couldn't say what it was. When I shared the good news, some people would listen and some would disagree, and it helped me in understanding what the Bible and the New Testament were all about.

I became very sure about my direction as a Christian and started thinking about getting baptized. By then I had thrown away my much-coveted pendant. In March 2008 I was baptized. Because I lived by myself in Singapore, there was nobody who objected to what I was doing, which was really good for me and made it possible to become a Christian in a fairly short time.

Orkud.com is similar to Facebook; in the same manner that you post about yourself, I quoted about my Saviour in the "Status" page and my religion status had changed from Hinduism to Christianity, so every one of my friends and relatives who saw it told my parents, and that was the bomb that exploded. It was also the easiest way to tell my parents about the change of my ways. By then my studies were over (March 2008), and I was looking for a job.

At that time there was a recession, and it was difficult for a foreigner to find a job in Singapore. I asked myself: "I believe in God with all my heart; all my friends, who are unbelievers, have jobs, and I'm having such a hard time finding a job—why am I going through all these difficulties?" I spoke to my Christian friends and leaders in the church, and the only answers I received were: "Keep on praying."

I kept praying and didn't lose my hope, and I was really sure that the Lord was taking His own time to give what was best for me. I got a small job as a restaurant manager in a small independent restaurant. It took four months to find that job. I was not happy with it, because I was working twelve hours a day for a low salary, but I kept my faith in the Lord and was still really sure that there was a reason why I started with a job I didn't like. I was concerning myself with repaying my student loan and, at the same time in India, my mother was crying and disappointed about my change to Christianity, and she kept sending me emails. Her main issue was my sister's marriage and that she may not find a groom from a good family because of my change, and that my father's dignity was touched as he lost face with other people. My answer to this was: "This is my personal belief, and it will not affect my family in any way. I told you about my belief in Jesus Christ, and it will in no way affect your lives; it is very personal for me." I even received telephone calls from my uncles and aunts who were saying, "If you were a drunk or a pervert, it wouldn't bother us, but why did you have to become a Christian?" Then I had a conversation with the Holy Spirit, where in my troubled heart I would question why this had to happen, but He would assure me not to worry, that God is a good God. So this reply gave me hope.

I received a better job offer from Pan Pacific hotel and took it. The experience I had acquired at the restaurant helped me to succeed as a supervisor in my new job, which also helped me to understand that even if, as a Christian, you go through difficulties that you don't understand, it is often a path to better things in the future.

Then my dear friend Emmy got an offer for a job in Australia, and she was already in the last steps of the application process. When she told me, I was stunned for a moment, and then I immediately proposed to her, and she replied, "Let's be friends." When Emmy told her mom, the latter was very scared and said no because of the repercussion she might suffer from my Hindu family. Nevertheless, Emmy couldn't resist my charms and my proposal and eventually broke down and said yes! She dropped her application to Australia and started to look for work in Singapore. We were looking for other openings around the world, as we wanted to relocate from Singapore, where the cost of living is very high and incomes very low. Emmy's friend heard about permanent residence in Canada; we went to meet a Canadian immigration lawyer who told us it would cost $10,000 for his fee, which was not affordable for us. We prayed and started applying directly online. The Lord proved faithful by granting us a visa within six months, which came as a total shock to us. We married before leaving for Canada. Neither side of our families knew of our marriage yet. We wanted to tell them that we wanted to get married in India before leaving for Canada, and I told my mom that I was in love with Emmy. My mom was very disappointed, and there were a lot of issues. As a Hindu there are lots of rituals to take care of, and as Christians of course we couldn't participate in them. Then my dad got involved and said that if the marriage were to take place, it had to be the Hindu way. I spoke to Emmy's family, and they said that if there was no other way, "Let it be like that." They also gave me a warning that this would be the one and only time. About two hundred believers prayed for us, and as a result my father called me and told us that if we didn't like to marry the Hindu way, we could get marry any way we liked, as long as it wasn't Christian. In the common interest for all, we thought of getting registered and holding a reception for everyone. My relatives said that nobody was going to attend, because it was an intercaste marriage. I said it was not a problem and that we would keep it in our prayers. When we reached India they gave Emmy an unexpected warm welcome, and we saw God's work in that. About 1,500 people came to the reception!

In India we went to different local churches, both in my hometown and in Emmy's, without the knowledge of my parents. I was able to give my Christian testimony. All the church members were very excited to know my name, because it has Krishna in it, the name of a Hindu god; all wanted to know my story. In the church I felt the closeness of people that we didn't feel in foreign Christian churches. Here in India, Christian churches really speak about family matters. Believers are therefore very close to each other and care for each other.

If something has to be done, or problems go through my life, I look forward to it, as I know I have a very powerful tool through prayer. And this is where and when I hear God's voice.

To be very frank, we went to different churches in Vancouver. In most of the churches, there are different groups of people sitting together by their ethnicity, and none of the groups will talk to the others. In one church we received a very warm welcome from the first time they saw us. After about three weeks, however, we found that nobody really wanted to speak to us. People would just greet us and turn away. Compared to India, where if I had a problem, whether financial or in need of moral support, a brother would immediately come alongside to help. If we were without a house, some people would immediately offer to share their home. So the Christians there behave truly as family; people are very open toward each other. On the other hand, if someone, for instance, is doing something wrong, here we won't tell that person anything. In India somebody will immediately speak to that person in a caring way and encourage that person to do what is right.

CHAPTER 5

The Idol Slayer

We live in a world that, to the same extent that it more and more rejects the Christian faith, also fabricated for itself more and more idols. ... And I believe that Christians have an enormous service to render to humankind in smashing these idols.—Andrew Goddard, *Idolatry: False Producers in the Bible*

We have established that anything or anyone is a potential idol the moment it diverts our affection from God. And, deep down, none of us desires to suffer bondage and intentionally act against the will of our Lord.

To avert the danger of something or someone becoming an idol, and to slay any idol that besets us, we must resist that object of our obsession and put it in its rightful place. There are ways with which we can redeem the good while rejecting the temptations the Enemy places in our path.

It is comforting that Paul states in Romans 7:18b–20, 24: "For I have the desire to do what is right, but not the ability to carry it out. For I do not do the good I want, but the evil I do not want is what I keep on doing. Now if I do what I do not want, it is no longer I who do it, but sin that dwells within me. ... Wretched man that I am! Who will deliver me from this body of death?"

Here is this champion of God who admits that although he delights in the laws of God, his inner being is constantly at war *for* or *against* sin.

In our human condition, our broken, sinful state will be with us until we move from this world into the eternal kingdom and into the presence of the Lord. "Then what's the point of resisting?" we may ask; it is in this: we can relate to Paul when he cries out, "Wretched man that I am! Who will deliver me from this body of death?" But Paul does not end there; then comes his jubilant shout: "Thanks be to God through Jesus Christ our Lord! So then, I myself serve the law of God with my mind, but with my flesh I serve the law of sin." And this is our ultimate consolation: that faced with this tension, through Christ we can overcome, because He has overcome death and the power of sin. No longer do we have to bow to sin.

When an idol is named, it is no longer hidden. It takes courage to name one's idol(s). The first step is to acknowledge an idol so that it can be dealt with, and the road to recovery and forgiveness can be taken. None of us likes to hear that our hearts might be captive to one or more idols. When an idol is identified, our instinct is to deny its existence. When those close to us identify an idol that has taken hold of us, we owe it to Christ and our fellow believers to heed the warning and take the admonitions seriously. We may not feel that others have the right to question what they perceive as an idol that has taken hold of us. However, that's not entirely true; God has that right, and God's kingdom is too important to let hindrances prevent us from fully proclaiming it. Moreover, taking to heart the warnings helps us to stay on the right course and accountable to fellow believers and God.

There is no easy road, and it will be hard work; it will be a long, arduous road. To deal with those idols that have stolen the affection owed to God will be a struggle, but it needs to be fought, and fought to the end. The good news is that the idol slayer par excellence is our Lord Jesus Christ, who overcame idols and, if allowed, will work through us to defeat ours. In Hebrews 12:4 (NIV), Paul admonishes us: "In your struggle against sin you have not yet resisted to the point of shedding your blood." He encourages us not to grow weary or fainthearted. Why should we be involved in this fight? For one, it is a testimony to nonbelievers. Although as Christians we are no longer part of this world, we are still very much in it and should influence it in a way that brings God's shalom. In 1 Corinthians 5:9–10 Paul warns us that we are not to associate with those who say they are Christians but whose lives are diametrically opposed to God's scriptural principles. Then Paul adds that to those of the world, we should be salt and light. The latter should be manifest in how we lead our lives, not according to the tyranny of the greater culture, but by redeeming culture through modest and thoughtful choices. We must plainly see with both our hearts and our will what Paul means when he says, "For we do not wrestle against flesh and blood, but against the rulers, against the authorities, against the cosmic powers over this present darkness, against the spiritual forces of evil in the heavenly places" (Ephesians 6:12, ESV).

With this knowledge, the implication is that we are waging a spiritual battle. Paul tells us that we have "not resisted until [we] shed blood"; he does not of course mean that we should take up arms against those who oppose Christianity. Paul, knowing how easy it is give in to the relentless attacks from the enemy camp, spurs us on to stand strong in the spiritual temptations until the enemy relinquishes. These spiritual attacks can be so intense that resisting at all cost may feel as if we shed blood. Therefore, in Ephesians 6:11 he entreats us to "put on the whole armour of God, that you [we] may be able to stand against the schemes of the devil" in order to do this battle against sin in spiritual warfare.

God's armour, His protection, His strength are ours when we choose to serve and obey Him. It requires our single-mindedness and determination in the face of temptation and distraction, a knowledge of and belief in Jesus' promises that He carries the yoke with us and that His yoke is light, and that He "will never leave us or forsake us" (Hebrews 13:5, NRSV). Jesus knows that we cannot overcome this spiritual battle on our own. By being yoked with Him, the burden of temptation and of resistance weakens so that we can persevere and stand strong.

When we accepted God's gift of salvation, we did so on faith; in other words, we believed from the heart. It follows that believing every promise of divine assistance and comfort needs to also move from an intellectual understanding to an acceptance of the heart, followed by a submission of the will. The knowing of those promises has to spring from deep within our being. No matter how many sermons we hear, enjoy, and agree with intellectually, they remain dead works without real redemptive and transforming faith. As long as our believing remains an intellectual exercise, the heart remains unmoved. Most of us have become inured and blind to this condition. How many of us can genuinely say that we have put what was heard in a sermon into action? Or was it that the pinch of conviction that was felt was soon forgotten and that life continued as before? We need to recommit, to break this stalemate and genuinely repent from our religiosity. There is no other way. Without ongoing renewal, our Christian walk is or becomes mere ritual and is a mockery of what being a Christian means in actuality. To follow Christ is costly, Dietrich Bonhoeffer wrote, "When Christ calls a man, He bids him come and die."[23]

Unless we slay our idols, by God's grace and strength, we cannot call ourselves Christians. A former Muslim who converted to Christianity said, "A Christian without a testimony is not a Christian!" He did not imply that a testimony is sharing of one's faith, the gospel, and the Four Spiritual Laws, but rather he meant that one's way of life is a testimony. His was a very sobering assertion.

Let us consider what redemption would look like if our choices were imbued by a concern for kingdom values. We would be ever vigilant that we not fall into a religious piety that is far removed from true obedience to and worship of God. Our obedience would not depend on living in a Christian subculture, but would rather be a full immersion in life without compromise to the standards of Christ. Bonhoeffer was of the opinion that only by living completely in this world could one learn to have faith, embracing all the duties and aspects that living in this world, while not of this world, entailed. Such obedience is difficult to achieve in our individualistic society. We desperately need one another to spur each other on and help each other up when we fall. We can overcome the enemy as brother helping brother and sister helping sister by the grace of God.

Among the idols identified, some merit particular attention because of their prevalence in our present society: parental coddling, technology, earning in order to consume more, entertainment and recreation.

Resisting Parental Coddling

Surely this can't be an idol? How could this be anything but right? Well, for one thing, Millennial parents are faced with the dilemma of dealing with children that have been growing up in a coddled environment, or they are guilty of creating this coddled environment. Coddling is the opposite of nurturing. In coddling, parents tend to be overprotective and indulgent.

Parents who nurture encourage their children to develop and grow, while providing healthy boundaries. In both cases parents love their children.

Parents who coddle their children want to shield them from any unpleasant experience. They try to protect their children from any possible danger. At the same time, wanting to spare their children pain often drives their concern; it hurts to see their children suffer. Yet children need to experience difficulties in order to learn how to deal with them. A coddling parental love tends to be idolatrous, as it puts the children before anyone and anything else.

Parents who nurture their children also wish to spare their children pain but understand that healthy development requires going through difficulties and overcoming them. The world does not revolve around the children, and the children learn appropriate respect for their parents and those in authority.

To some extent, secular experts have been advocating discussion and reasoning with children starting at a very early age. Any form of corporal punishment, even a healthy reprimand, is viewed by many as a thing of the past. This often brings parental authority into question, and we see more and more children ruling the roost. Such advice has contributed to parents thinking that shielding their children from harm is the way to move forward. We can appreciate that as the pendulum has swung from one extreme to the other, parents feel that they have to constantly occupy their children, who, in turn, due to the unrelenting stimuli, instead of learning to develop particular interests, have a very short attention span and skip from one activity to the next, from one topic to the other, without being able to focus for longer periods of time. Parents become facilitators who must keep their children amused; they become part of the entertainment module, as children set the rules of the household. Moreover, since children are introduced to computers and computer games at an increasingly younger age, their minds are constantly being bombarded with changing input and data, which may negatively affect their ability to concentrate.

Christian parents are not immune to the secular influences that dictate how parents should raise their children. Society takes a dim view of parents who seek to raise their children according to biblical models. The pressure on parents to adopt the secular notion of raising children should not be underestimated.

But what is a parent to do? After being stretched to the limits after working a whole day, it is overwhelming to then have to attend to household chores. No wonder computer games save the day. A friend of mine calls this childcare by electronics. This could very well be the fallout of instituting laws that prevent parents from exercising healthy authority and discipline. We cannot, and should not, turn back the clock, but at the same time as Christian parents we need to find a way to promote godly discipline where the child is seen as special in the eyes of the Lord and also in need of firm boundaries. We cannot expect children to fully comprehend a given situation when we try to reason with the child.

What scriptural recourse do we parents have in raising our children? Auspiciously, discernment and wisdom are gifts that we may liberally call upon, since God promises to make those available when we ask Him. Throughout Psalms and Proverbs wisdom is praised, and in our present age it is something that we Christians and parents in particular must hunger for. How else can we guide our children in ways that keep them from the Evil One and in the ways that God has decreed bring life? Suffice it to say that each of us must purpose to raise our children in a sound, godly manner, rather than in a sentimental, romantic notion of what Christian godliness looks like. Memorizing Scripture is helpful in developing biblical knowledge but does not produce a godly character unless tied to a disciplined life with boundaries that help children discern what is good and healthy when faced with the desires dictated by secular and Christian commercialism. Living outward lives, lives that prepare them to think of the other rather than of themselves, will ground them in selfless and sacrificial living.

When children learn to see that not everything revolves around themselves, that there are others we need to be mindful of, their focus can shift from the self to the other. As parents, we need to show our children the importance of living for one another. Children can find joy in giving and sharing by, for instance, helping prepare a dessert to bring to an elder person.

Children's natural talents can be turned into benefits to be shared with others. They learn to be accountable to others through their God-given gifts.

For children to learn a balanced life, it is important that parents set the tone. When sharing with others, enjoying others' company, doing acts of kindness for another, a child will soon accept this way of life as good and right.

On the other hand, children need to learn to own up to mistakes they have made or hurts they have caused. When a child admits a shortcoming and receives forgiveness, the child can learn the value of honesty and forgiveness.

When it comes to technology, when parents model healthy attitudes, it will be much easier for the children to follow suit. Parents who have learned to set boundaries on uses of technology will have children who can learn to use technology wisely. They will understand that being present with others is more important than allowing the distraction of their need to stay wired. They learn to set priorities when choosing between people and things.

Proverbs 22:1 (RSV) tells us, "A good name is to be chosen rather than great riches, and favor is better than silver or gold." That goes against everything that our Western culture promotes in today's values. The well-known Proverb 22:6 (RSV) promises us, "Train up a child in the way he should go, and when he is old he will not depart from it." When we parents lead by example and train our children in the way God intended, we may be assured that children will stay the course. When we parents have done all we could by the grace of God, with the intention to raise our children with godly values, we may not always see the immediate fruit of our labour. A child may still experiment during teen years, but the Lord will see to it that this child will return home, because a child is conscious of God's voice. It is comforting to know that the love God has for all of his creatures is far above the love any mother and father has for her or his children. Admitting our powerlessness and lack of resources—as humans—is a first step to allowing God to help us raise our children in the fear and awe of the Lord. They will become Kingdom citizens whose lives will truly develop into Ambassadors of Christ bringing others to reconciliation with God (2 Corinthians 5:20). What relief we parents can find in knowing, believing and trusting the promises of God, even if a child seems to take a detour that may be harmful. It requires that we submit to God's guidance in rearing our children. Proverb 29:17 persuades us to: "Discipline your son, and he will give you rest; he will give delight to your heart." A child left to his devices, grows up willful, unthankful and at risk, while we may have the confidence that the opposite is true when we heed God's recommendation.

Another challenge for us is to recognize our own level of enculturation that has moved us far afield from living according to God's principles. Our task as today's parents is anything but easy; it requires a transformation in our perspective of what differentiates true from false Christianity that can be discerned only through Scripture. We need to guard against appearing pious. We need to build our faith by feeding on Scripture, and by being rooted in prayer. Only then we shall have the confidence of raising our children in a way that God intended.

Wise counsel and much prayer will move parents from unhealthy coddling to healthy nurturing. If we are serious about the spiritual and physical future of our children and our children's children, we will willingly acquire a new divine paradigm and will have the courage to tackle this responsibility. We can find strength in knowing that God has gifted us with children in the first place, they are His, and He is counting on us to do our part.

Redeeming Techno Idols

It is amazing how technology has stolen our affection without our noticing it.

A major distracting and odious aspect of technology is its insidiousness; while it may be excused in a secular world, it behooves Christians to be mindful of it. It is commonplace to see Christians playing with devices such as smart phones, browsing online or texting someone with astonishing nonchalance during a sermon and prayer time. What drives this seemingly insatiable need to use these gadgets at inappropriate times? Has attention span become so atrophied that having our full focus on the matter at hand has become impossible? Does our need not to miss anything make us unable to grasp when these distractions and interruptions are inappropriate? The same applies to our need to not miss out on anything, which translates into a flippancy communicated by a disregard for the speakers and towards prayer: "This is really too boring to give it my time to." Through our technology, we have lost our sense of boundaries and common courtesy.

Leaning over to my web-browsing pew neighbour, I whispered, "I hope you're looking for Jesus," which triggered an immediate switching off of the device; he fully understood the implied message. I wasn't trying to embarrass him, but his reaction indicated that he knew full well this was not an appropriate time or place to engage his social network.

True enough, while many of us may not be preoccupied with our gadgets, it could very well be that our hearts and minds are quite in another place while our bodies try to pose a pious listening stance. To be sure, the latter is as disrespectful as the former in a way that is invisible to others (but not to God!), while the first cannot be missed by its inescapable presence. Regardless, such habits reinforce our lack of interest for, and intimacy with, God. Our innovative devices, rather than being tools used to enrich others, have become distractions that keep us from growing spiritually and emotionally. They become barriers between God and us.

When we are more aware of how Satan ever attempts to turn good things, such as technology, into harmful pursuits, we will not allow him to sidetrack us into creating harmful and selfish habits. When we are mindful of the Devil's tactics, we can guard against slipping into destructive dependency and inappropriate attitudes.

In the end, what is it that matters? Is not our coming together on Sunday for the purpose of worshipping God with one another? To give God thanks for the week we completed in His grace and to request His presence in the new week ahead?

Os Guinness speaks about the "sinful imagination of our hearts" and how these imaginations are "the supreme idol-making factory."[24] By ignoring this "sinful imagination," we have opened ourselves up to the idols that become entrenched in our daily lives. A case in point is George, who as a youth became so involved with computers and online gaming that they eventually consumed more than twelve hours in a day. He had cut himself off from the rest of his family and had only a couple of friends, who shared in the same excesses; their moods were sullen. He was neglecting healthy eating and sleeping habits. When his mother would try to reason with him, and once even removed the computer while he was at school, he would become physically violent and angry with her. George was in total denial at how this technology had become his addiction and idol, how it was ruining him and the lives of those around him. By the grace of God,

George came to a point where he realized his compulsive behavior and its consequences. He is not entirely free from the hold that gaming had on him, and he will probably struggle with both the temptation and the idol for the rest of his life; he has to constantly depend on God's grace and remind himself how important it is to maintain a balance.

With such onslaughts on our minds, how can we possibly overcome? In our own strength we will surely fail, and this is exactly why Jesus had to die and rise again to demonstrate to all that He is victor; He has indeed overcome the powers of darkness and the idolatrous tendencies of the heart. Mobile devices, computers, and televisions are now so intricately woven into our daily lives that the need to be alert to these potential idols is critical. To determine our dependency, keeping a log may reveal where, when, and how much time is spent being consumed by technology. This means being brutally honest with ourselves and with others as we take inventory. It goes without saying that not all of our time spent with technology is wrong or bad. It is the overattachment or unbalanced affection towards these distractions that takes us away from meaningful interaction with those we love or with those we are tasked with (nonbelievers) and from God. Our transformation will arise naturally out of an inner renewal that only Christ can effect.

In the 1998 article of *The Plough* magazine, ~~chrisz@bruderhof.com~~ stated:

> We're so swamped with options of easy communication that on many days there's no *need* to meet another human being face to face at all. ...
>
> The Bruderhof has had e-mail for three years, and its enslaving convenience has not brought us new energy, but new fatigue. E-mail has neither heightened our productivity nor improved our relationships. Instead of aiding us in responding more effectively to the mind-boggling onslaught of information that comes to our door each day, it has mostly paralyzed us and left us wondering where to begin. ... It also made us realize that

we could remove the occasion for such headaches. ~~We could unplug.~~[25]

(strikethrough and emphasis by *The Plough* author)

Only by standing in the strength and mercies of God and in proclaiming to the Enemy and to ourselves that Christ conquered "the powers of darkness and of the air" will we overcome our idols. We should desire a return to community and family life. Our individualistic society, of which we are very much a part, has caused not only familial and societal fragmentation but also a sense that what we do, the struggles we have, the sins we want to overcome, can all be resolved in the privacy of our own personal world. The collateral damage is the guilt flowing out of unconfessed and secret sins that we try to deal with in our own strength. We so need one another, as mentioned in Proverbs 27:17 (NRSV): "As iron sharpens iron, so a person sharpens his friend." In Ecclesiastes 4:12 (NIV) we are told that there is strength in numbers: "Though one may be overpowered, two can defend themselves. A cord of three strands is not quickly broken."

Quentin Schultze submits that

> moral vision grows out of a community that accepts responsibility for a place and time, not out of lone tourists traveling through cyberspace in hopes of getting the best deal on the latest product advocating their two cents worth. Instant messaging and online plebiscites without an ennobling moral vision are poor substitutes for real communities of moral discourse.[26]

We must also recognize that the opposite causes more fragmentation in relationships; we may well make new friends online, but at what cost to those close to us? Shultze suggests that, "information technology provides a way for individuals to escape their current social relationships and enter into new relationships that redefines who they are."[27] Such can alienate loved ones from one another or justify the breakdown of a relationship. Sadly, by valuing the online relationships more than those present in the now, it is easy to find justification that new online friends understand us better than our spouse or our parents, ultimately magnifying the rift with those we should be committed to. But therein lies the deception. Online friends are not emotionally invested, because these are relationships of convenience. Schultze explains that, opposite to a cyber-community,

> Locale is also the setting for *hospitality,* one of the most important neighborly traditions among many cultures. Acts of hospitality reflect some classical virtues, including the *courage* to open one's home to people who are different from us, the *love* that leads us to share with others, and the *wisdom* to respect another's wishes and preferences.[28]

It is precisely these neighbourly acts that should make us different from the secular person. Besides, these are not just optional things; as true followers of Christ, we are commanded to be hospitable and to share with strangers. The physical connections are what keep us grounded and accountable to one another.

The Trinity is the ultimate example of community. While Jesus walked among us, everything He did was relational. When he sought seclusion it was to pray and commune with the Father.

By physically spending time with one another and setting aside our technology, we show our love for others and affirm their worth. By extending, for instance, impromptu lunch invitations after a church service, to people we are not familiar with, we open our homes and hearts to our neighbours. Making people our priority over our smartphones and other gadgets demonstrates to them how important they are in God's sight.

To reclaim what the Enemy has stolen, whenever we feel the compulsive urge to unnecessarily check our email, go online, or text someone, let us pause and ask ourselves: *Is this the best use of my time right now? Who benefits? Will this take face-to-face time away from my spouse, children, friends or others? What kingdom values do my actions have?* If the answer is unfavourable, then the activity should be postponed. In response, we could take an intentional twenty-four hour break from all technological distractions by turning off the cell phone, postponing messaging, emailing, and engaging in social media. "Leave my computer turned off? I can't!" you scream. "My work needs to be able to get in touch with me!" But is that really so? Is the job a 24/7 situation? Were we created to function 24/7? As an example, secular labour laws in democratic countries have instituted limits to the workday and provide one full day per week of rest, and region-specific mandates provide other guidelines.[29] Should we not do better?

"But . . . I need to get a hold of my kids!" you may counter. How did we cope before SMS, cell phones and personal computers? In our technological infancy we managed to stay connected. Today is it an addiction that is talking? The disproportionate need to constantly be within reach has at times overpowered all our senses to the point of absurdity. This feeling alone demonstrates the manner in which these technologies turn into idols. We are no longer in control of these technologies; the technologies have become our masters, and we their slaves. How can such conditions promote kingdom values? Let's give these inanimate objects their proper place and redeem them through judicious and measured use so that the technologies can be our allies and at our service. Changes, even small ones, will be constructive, and within Christian communities we can hearten one another to persevere.

Whom can we call, and what buddy system can we create, to wean ourselves from unhealthy attachments to technologies? Who will be there to cheer us on as we reclaim our personhood as it was designed in the image of God? Surrounding ourselves with trusted loved ones and friends will encourage us to stay the course as we break the bonds of our technologies. Overcoming our addictions involves entering into a covenant with someone willing to walk with us on this journey, praying for strength, and sitting in God's presence with thankfulness.

Even children are suffering the repercussions of our technological age. As an example some time ago, three families gathered to celebrate a family member's milestone. As the children sat together, it was fascinating to watch them together and at the same time alone. Each was playing an electronic game, and each was intent on the screen before him and her. There was neither connection nor interaction among these children; it was baffling. Is this how we as Christian families are supposed to live out kingdom values? Of course not. In the measure that we have lost touch with God, we need to reconnect with Him and allow our deepest yearnings to be satisfied by Him. We need to reclaim the art of playing together;

of exploring nature and of going on an adventure, of just plain spending undivided time with one another.

Confronting the Idolatry of Earning and Consuming More

If the false gods of money, technology and entertainment imprison the world, how much of this has rubbed off on Christians in the West?

We no longer have to stand in line to be served or purchase our goods face-to-face; this makes us increasingly anonymous and keeps us in greater isolation. One of the consequences is that this anonymity removes any responsibility towards others. If I don't see the person I'm buying from, I don't feel obligated to act fairly. I may, for instance, falsely criticize a merchant or berate an employee when providing online reviews. Since we are invisible to one another, I don't feel the same sense of responsibility and fairness I would have when interacting in person. The plethora of online offerings represents a double-edged sword. On one hand it can be helpful for many who may not have the time to go out and shop at the end of a busy workday. On the other hand, online shopping may prove too seductive for those who might succumb to the addiction of compulsive buying. One click leads to another, and some items we may not normally consider announce themselves as great bargains if bought *now*. These myriad choices at allegedly special prices are enticing. For some of us they become a snare that promises fulfillment but never delivers. Consumption may offer a temporary feel-good effect that quickly vanishes and urges us to keep buying. In this sense, consumption takes our soul and is a false image of what real necessities are.

As a result, whether online or in person, consuming to excess has enslaved our society, and we as Christians have not been immune to its call. Not only has consuming reached epidemic proportions, but so has the drive to earn more in order to achieve desirable lifestyles according to secular standards. The two invariably go together.

What kingdom values do we live out by shopping and acquiring without restraint? How does this honour God? How much happier do we feel when we have gone on a shopping spree? Does it satisfy at the end of the day? Does it take care of the craving for the next new thing? What example are we setting for the next generations? When is enough, enough?

This is best expressed in Shania Twain's song "Ka-Ching," in which she sings that shopping and the mall have become our religion and that we spend beyond our means.[30]

The drive to shop for things even when we don't have the means has reached colossal proportions, yet people continue to charge their credit cards, with the consequence of going deeper and deeper into debt, all to satisfy an insatiable need to possess.

The extent to which we can define our attachment to material possession and wealth will be the measure of our healthy or disproportionate affection for things.

In our pursuit for financial and material happiness, Goudzwaard warns us that

> In the name of material prosperity we have yielded our
> responsibility to the perceived source of our prosperity.
> Unchallenged economic growth, an idol made by our own
> hands, has become a power which forces its will on us:
> Christians and non-Christians alike, *possessed by an end*
> (material prosperity), have allowed various forces, means,
> and powers in our society (for instance untrammelled
> economic growth) to rule over us as gods.[31]

We no longer see God as our only source of provision, and the work we do as a gift from Him. We have become so accustomed to the secular ideology that proclaims we can do anything we set our minds to, that God has become a tagline at the end of a prayer or a pious mention in a conversation. In our prayers we do not really believe in our hearts that God hears our every sigh, petition and thanks. Hence, we pursue material life and our right to enjoyment lustily—as long as we do not sin too blatantly. Alas, enculturation in our pursuits is already a blatant sin; we just have not recognized it as such.

Os Guinness, in observing contemporary Christians, asserted five ironies:

> First, Protestants today need the most protesting and
> reforming, second, Evangelicals and fundamentalists have

become the most worldly tradition in the church; third, conservatives are becoming the most progressive. Fourth, Christians in many cases are the prime agents of their own secularization. Fifth, through its uncritical engagement with modernity, the church is becoming its own most effective gravedigger.[32]

It is exactly that uncritical engagement that we as Christians need to examine and turn away from. More public discourse at church and in fellowship groups needs to take place to address ways in which we can recognize when we are espousing the secular culture's values and are falling into the traps of idolatry. It is unfortunate that too many ministers, preachers, and teachers have been deceived into accepting the corrupted secular values and are leading many believers astray as a result. John Seel points out how, in America,

The evangelical identity shifted from being grounded in the source of blessing to being grounded in the blessing itself. Their status as pilgrims in search of the heavenly kingdom was less important than being citizens of a "Christian America." Following the pattern of most idolatry, something to be appreciated became a point of overattachment, a source of reliance, and finally an idol that led to public pride and self-deception. Jesus confronted this form of idolatry in people whose primary identity was in their Jewishness.[33]

By taking pride in our identity as Christians or Evangelicals, or whatever our Christian tribe may be, we do not realize that we have become proud of that status thus deceiving ourselves that we are better than "those in the world"; we have been sideswiped by the Enemy. The irony is that we have not felt the blow from the attack, and hence we think all is well.

While in some parts of the world people suffer the outrage of injustice and oppression and grinding poverty, in the West we have been subjected to the injustice of workaholism, of mass production, of meaningless labour (such as factory workers performing the same repetitive tasks day after day) and of insignificance (where our work is perceived as has having little or no worth) in order to satisfy our lifestyles.

It is clear that income as an idol, so as to acquire and consume, is no less idolatrous than the opulent and decadent lifestyle of the Roman Empire at the time of Jesus. When telling the Parable of the Sower, He warns us "the cares of the world and the deceitfulness of riches and the desires for other things enter in and choke the word, and [the seed] proves unfruitful" (Mark 4:19, ESV).

The danger of worrying or obsessing over daily matters and pursuits is that they ultimately rob us from a vibrant spiritual life. When we are preoccupied by these matters, even the Word we hear preached on Sundays, or on radio and television broadcasts, is choked and does not find root in our heart. Our heart is too full with worldly pursuits and has no room for deeper spiritual life and meaning. There is just no room left for the Holy Spirit to ground us in the truths that will carry us into the kingdom of God. We deceive ourselves if we think otherwise. God warns us time and again because He knows how insidious and all-consuming those deceptive idols are. Wealth and consumption leave us dissatisfied, malcontent, empty, and lonely. They instill in us a feeling of envy towards those who obtain what we could not, and throw us in a relentless cycle of unsatisfied desires.

Paul says, in Philippians 4:11–12 (NIV) : "I have learned to be content whatever the circumstances. I know what it is to be in need, and I know what it is to have plenty. I have learned the secret of being content in any and every situation, whether well fed or hungry, whether living in plenty or in want." This is precisely the crux of the matter: contentment. Our consumer society does not want us in a state of contentment. It defines contentment as that new car, shiny computers, and such. Real contentment rests in accepting that what we have, or where we are, is adequate.

Paul tells us in no uncertain terms, "Those who desire to be rich fall into temptation, into a snare, into many senseless and harmful desires that plunge people into ruin and destruction" (1 Timothy 6:9, ESV). Not a very encouraging prospect, contrary to some of the North American health-and-prosperity theologies that have been taking the Americas and even parts of Africa by storm. When Jesus tells us that he came to give us life, and life more abundantly (John 10:10), he did not mean that He came to give us more material things and a life of ease and comfort. Why else would He say that if the world hated Him, it would hate His followers also? We have to ask ourselves how much we believe in what Jesus told us. Do we truly believe Him? When He said that we couldn't serve two masters, God and our earthly desires, how is it that we think we can? We will either despise one and be totally devoted to the other, but we cannot have affection for both (Matthew 6:24). To disagree with His pronouncement would be actually admitting that we believe Jesus to be a liar, else we think Him old-fashioned and that He was only speaking to those of that day. In such a case, it would be better that we did away with Christ altogether and stop pretending to be His followers.

As Christians we have failed to notice the signs of spiritual erosion in our own pursuit of material accumulation, pleasure, comforts. and ease. It is crucial that we become once again intentional in our listening, reading, writing and texting to recognize this insidious erosion. We hear some of our own pundits promote that wealth and prosperity are a blessing from the Lord, and something we are entitled to strive for.

One secular broadcaster on a respected Canadian national channel promotes his financial show by quipping to his partner, "Greed is good and I love money!" It may sound funny and harmless; in fact, it is an in-your-face blatant disregard for values that encourage caring for one another. It is an attitude that derides Jesus' intrinsic principle of caring for and respecting all creatures. Even if the program offered solid financial advice, our watching it makes us party to this person's values and morals.

Our participation in secular wisdom may be that we so hunger to see God at work in our midst that we feel the need to help Him along because we want to experience His blessings, be they material, health or spiritual. Yet to claim our Christian right to be blessed, we rely on our own ability to pray and recite the right "formulae." The world's self-reliance and self-actualization is so deeply ingrained in our Christian walk that we don't see that in fact we are anything but reliant on God. By wanting our material blessings now, we live on our terms, no longer following His plan, and move further away from the kingdom of God. It is my conviction that we Western Christians have either totally given up taking God's Word at face value or are using His Word as a magic formula to obtain health and prosperity and other selfish requests; all equally wrong and heretical.

Os Guinness exhorts, "By all means plunder freely of the treasures of modernity, but in God's name make sure that what comes out of the fire that will test our life's endeavours is gold, fit for the temple of God and not a late twentieth-century image of a Golden Calf."[34]

The service we must render to one another, then, is to dare to challenge these heretical beliefs that have been widely accepted without question by Christians. Sure, the Scriptures are full of passages where God blessed His people through riches because of their obedience to His statutes. Nevertheless, when Jesus came He changed the paradigm and turned everything upside down. The blessing Jesus talks about ensues from loving one another and serving one another. No longer would riches be a sign of God's blessing on our obedience, but rather we are told to follow Jesus, who did not have a place to rest his head, and receive blessing upon blessing through acts of faith and obedience. The New Testament blessings are spiritual in nature rather than material. In Ephesians, Paul speaks of how God has blessed us in Christ "with every spiritual blessing in the heavenly places" (1:3, ESV). God's promise that in Abraham the nations would be blessed extends to Christians (Galatians 3:8–9). Jesus declares blessed those who believe in Him though they have not seen Him (John 10:29). All who are Jesus' followers are called blessed when they suffer for His name's sake and endure suffering for believing in Him (James 1:12). Jesus spoke of blessings at the Sermon on the Mount (Matthew 5:3–10; Luke 6:20–22). These blessings are lasting and culminate in eternal togetherness with God.

Jesus tells us following Him would cost us, but at the same time His yoke is easy and His burden light (Matthew 11:30). If we want to live entirely according to the Old Testament blessings, it follows that we must follow the Old Testament rules, and then we cannot expect to live under God's grace offered in Christ. May we therefore be quick to urge one another towards virtuous living, not by moralizing but by keeping each other fully aware of the dangers we risk if we do not stay close to Jesus. Paul entreats us: "exhort one another every day, as long as it is called 'today,' that none of you may be hardened by the deceitfulness of sin" (Hebrews 3:12, ESV). Sin, idolatry, is difficult to roust once it has taken residence in our hearts. The outcome is that we become hardened; indifferent, even immune to God's loving guidance and discipline. No wonder Jesus grew frustrated and asked whether He would find faith when He returned to Earth. Yet God with His infinite mercy commands that we keep our lives "free from love of money, and be content with what [we] have, for he has said, 'I will never leave you nor forsake you'" (Hebrews 13:5, ESV); even as He commands us, He promises us that He will never abandon us.

Craig M. Gay concludes by suggesting that

> It may also help to juxtapose the modern obsession with acquisition, grasping and possessing with the Christian values of gratitude, generosity and hope. Far from encouraging us to accumulate and / or consume as much as we possibly can, the Scriptures exhort us to view our lives as a gracious gift from God for which we are to be grateful. We are further exhorted to express our gratitude by giving ourselves generously away in the love of God and in the love of our neighbour (see 1Tim. 6:18).[35]

We have not been created for this world, which is temporal, but for a world and a kingdom that will have no end, and where everything will be restored to wholeness without sin and suffering. It is that world that we need to keep in sight so that we do not give in to the lure of temporal and perishing things. As Jacques Ellul puts it, "The victory of Christ through the cross means that *the powers have been despoiled*. Material things have therefore again become mere things. This desacralized world without idols is not something that happens automatically as a result of the cross of Christ. It requires action on the part of those who have been united to the crucified Christ by baptism and faith."[36]

We must, as it were, become iconoclasts and radicals so that we can instil God's grace, life, and hope in a perishing and hopeless world. To achieve this we must regain our position in Christ and our calling as followers of the crucified and risen One who empowers us to slay the idols.

Reframing Entertainment and Recreation

Whenever we surf channels, be it online or on television, we are making an active decision to tacitly collaborate with either the powers of light or with the powers of evil. Neil Postman contended that

> the television screen itself has a strong bias toward a psychology of secularism. The screen is so saturated with our memories of profane events, so deeply associated with the commercial and entertainment worlds that it is difficult for it to be recreated as a frame for sacred events. ... The television screen wants you to remember that its imagery is always available for your amusement and pleasure. The television preachers themselves are well aware of this. They know that their programs do not represent a discontinuity in commercial broadcasting but are merely part of an unbroken continuum.[37]

How much more amusement can we stomach? Recreation, as God designed it, brings refreshment and restores us from the toil and stresses of everyday life. It is good. God rested on the seventh day of creation when He finished the work and pronounced the seventh day holy, a day of rest (Genesis 2:2–4). God did not create humanity to be bound in frenetic activity seven days a week.

While programs promote hero and celebrity worship, status and prestige, real people have in fact become quite irrelevant. To give our lives some meaning, we watch reality shows and vicariously live through those who dare to shamelessly exhibit themselves to the rest of the world. As a society we have become mere voyeurs and have lost any sense of decorum and appropriateness. To our disgrace, we have bought into an industry that serves up indecent meals for consumption to even the youngest viewers. Exemplary role models have, by and large, been replaced by celebrities who, for shock value and excitement, appear in modes of undress to such an extent that even parental viewers have lost their sense of boundaries and morality. The reality that what is served up has become the first stage of pornography is completely lost on viewers. Such values were not so aggressively promoted until the late twentieth century, not even in a secularized environment.

It may come as no surprise, then, that Christians from more traditional and modest cultures who have migrated to Western countries try to shield their children and youth from the onslaught of immoral images. They are often shocked at the permissiveness manifested among their Western fellow believers. We can only blame ourselves for the bad name the West receives because of the public display of immodesty. Because we live in the midst of it, we are unable to distinguish what they seem to observe so clearly.

We can, and must, redeem entertainment so that it reflects values that promote respect and are meaningful. Otherwise, as Neil Postman puts it: "Our politics, religion, news, athletics, education and commerce have been transformed into congenial adjuncts of show business, largely without protest or even much popular notice. The result is that we are a people on the verge of amusing ourselves to death."[38]

Entertainment can be provocative, humorous, or thrilling and at the same time modest and in good taste. It is up to us to seek and discover contemporary forms of entertainment that, secular or otherwise, are well written and engaging and maintain values that are not contrary and offensive to God's character. Christian artists should be encouraged to produce for a broader audience by creating works with substance, free of "Christianese" and Christian platitudes. As an expression of God's common grace, Christians should applaud wholesome art by secular and Christian artists alike, for the sake of the gifts God gave them.

This process requires active participation from artists and audiences alike. We must be willing to admit when something is poorly made or in poor taste and strive to produce art and entertainment that is solid and worth being experienced by all. Art should be provocative—as in thought-provoking—illuminating and deep, without settling for mediocre, sentimental work. When we experience exceptional work imbued with grace and creativity, devoid of self-seeking adulation and gratification, as Christians we should be the first ones to applaud, support, and promote such artists. A Christ-centered approach to art and entertainment will consequently free us to celebrate, laugh, and cry in ways that respect our Creator and bring hope to a lost society.

This we can do only through example. Proclaiming the gospel of Christ without a willingness to go against the cultural stream, through activities that harmonize with what we believe, will remain ineffective, irrelevant, and hypocritical.

Questions
1. Which one of the idols mentioned in this chapter do I react to strongest in anger and/or animosity?
2. Having identified my idol(s), am I willing to submit it/them to God and allow Him to truly be the Lord of my life?
3. If none of these apply to me, which can I list that captivate most or all of my time, energies, and affection?
4. In my family circle and circle of friends, whom can I enlist to be my buddy, to come alongside as, with God's grace, I cooperate with Christ's transforming power?
5. What weekly calls can I set up with my buddy to keep me accountable and on track?

(Take time to prayerfully make a list of those things the Holy Spirit brings to mind.)

Prayer
God, by your grace and with the help of your Holy Spirit, grant me the grace to be brutally and fearlessly honest with myself and with You, in identifying those areas that have become idols in my life.

Lord, alone I'm powerless to overcome this/these idol(s) in my life. Forgive me for putting other people/things/activities [*name the person(s), things and activities*] ahead of You. Grant me grace to daily stay the course in the power of Your son Jesus Christ, and resist the seductions of the Enemy.

Thank you for loving me as I am and for hearing my sighs and cries. I long to love You as You designed me to.

Tigist's Story
I grew up in a very small town in South Eastern Ethiopia. I came to Canada in 2005 because I married an Ethiopian Canadian. My parents

belong to a Protestant church where I grew up. I accepted Christ as my personal Savior when I was sixteen.

I accepted Christ because I felt that something was missing, and that I was not Christian enough, although I did lead a pure life, since I had been raised with strong values. In our circles we strictly live out Christianity. Worship, church, and Sunday worship cannot be missed; it would rank our Christianity as low level if we did. We obey the Bible in a strict but not legalistic way, with a lot of grace; and because of our love of Christ there is a lot of freedom and love. People may do whatever they like, but when they accept Christ they say, "These things and ways of life are now cut from me, and I now hate them; I cannot be like that anymore." The leadership leads with love, and those who attend and don't live according to Christian principles will be spoken to with kindness; these people are not abandoned to themselves. They are taught in the ways of the Lord and not thrown out of the church, but at the same time these people must know that a transformation needs to take place. For instance, if a preacher got divorced or became immoral, the church would teach him, lead him to reconcile. Nevertheless, if that person didn't give heed, this preacher would be able to continue to come but could no longer preach, unless he embraces the good thing, the right life, and witness according to the Scriptures. This would be true whether the preacher is theologically trained or simply a lay preacher.

I was living for my own spiritual and moral satisfaction and was only happy when I lived according to what is considered Christian, as stated in the Bible or as Jesus said. I didn't do it for the approval of others. Christians and non-Christians around me respected me and my beliefs. Even though the latter may not have accepted what I believe, they respected it, and I was a testimony to them, which led quite a few people to faith in Christ.

For me, I just have in my simplistic interpretation the Trinity: God the Father, the Son, and the Holy Spirit, the three in one. I mostly pray to God and conclude in the name of Jesus. But sometimes I call on the name of Jesus Christ. Mostly I pray to God and ask, for instance, "Holy Spirit, teach me, lead me to the truth."

One thing to guide me is the Holy Bible, which has an answer to everything in many ways and leads me to the truth. I also get a special feeling or way, especially when I pray, and I perceive that as the leading of the Holy Spirit: "The Spirit leads you in all truth" (John 16:13). Some things will press very strongly on my heart, and they don't go away until I do them. For instance, if I get very angry, my heart will say "Why are you angry? You have to learn to be patient," and it will press on me until I let it go. This is the Holy Spirit speaking to me, and I have to obey.

My feelings about Western Christianity are mixed. For the majority, I get confused when I compare it to what I practised or how I lived back home. I get shocked, for instance, regarding the whole issue of drunkenness among Christians. Sometimes I cannot see a difference between Christians and non-Christians regarding moral values. For example, in a Pentecostal church some couples were living together without being married. After a while I would see the marriage ceremony. This was shocking to me. What was the purpose of having a wedding covenant if they already lived together? This has become part of the church culture, and I'm afraid that this might be one of the reasons for having so many divorces here. If the marriage doesn't work out, Christians just divorce. They may then have a new partner and live together and so on. Just like the world. It is a form of immorality; although such people may appreciate those who are faithful to their vows, they're unable to live that way and according to divine principles. This is not common in my country. It's almost nonexistent because there is a stronger sense of Christian family.

Recently I read *The Story of Christianity*, which helped me to see that in the past, things were not like this in the West. I read that in the eighteenth and part of the nineteenth centuries the same Christian values existed that are in my home country today. Today, I don't see the same Christian values in North America and Europe as are present in my country. I don't believe Christianity is 100 percent destroyed. I believe there are quite a few that still have these values. For those who still hold on to the values, if I could meet those few, I would say to them, "Pray and work hard for God to bring back those godly values from before." If I get the chance to speak to the Christians who have walked away from those values, I would say: "Try to look for Jesus in a different way than you know Him now; look for the real Jesus, who touches inside and transforms. Pray; prayers work. You have been deceived in believing that how Christians live now is the right way. There is a different way, which you haven't identified yet and you would be more satisfied than you are now. You may be restless now; and yet you may think that you have God because you go to church; but you don't."

CHAPTER 6

Repenting and Returning to God

*Also many of those [in Ephesus] who became believers confessed
and disclosed their practices. A number of those who practiced
magic collected their books and burned them publicly; when
the value of these books was calculated, it was found to come
to fifty thousand silver coins. So the word of the Lord grew
mightily and prevailed.*—Acts 19:18–20

Many in Ephesus who surrendered to God were so cut to the
quick that they separated themselves from everything that was
idolatrous and opposed to God. It was not enough to get rid
of the books; they went a step further and burned them. In so doing
others would not be exposed to the ungodly nature of these books, thus
protecting them from the practice. Their decisive action demonstrated the
extent they were convicted of the sinful practices of their former lives. No
thought was given to the monetary value of what they were destroying; the
total of 50,000 silver coins was a considerable sum for those times. Most
Bible commentaries equate one coin (or one Attic drachma) to one day's
wage. It was a small fortune! These critical decisions serve as an example
of the kind of actions that should follow our own conversion, repentance,
and recommitment.

A weakness we face time and again is the human perspective we use to
view our faith or faithfulness. It is not so much the following of rules and
precepts that determines faith, but a sober appraisal of whose followers we

truly are. We are so used to hearing what rights we have, what we deserve, and so on, that we have forgotten on whose terms we are living and acting. We have endorsed most of the secular positions in these matters. This is exactly the rub of life, at least for followers of Christ. We know what we ought to do yet decide that it does not matter whether we follow the right course of action. Thus, we face the consequences of acting according to our own will and desires or choose to act according to God's terms, for the benefit of all. For every instance where we follow our own inclinations, we are deliberately choosing to do things on our terms, and against God and His will. Ultimately, in everyday decisions and actions the question we must intentionally ask ourselves is this: On whose terms am I going to proceed?

Because we have become so deeply entrenched in the dominant culture, we, as followers of Christ, have a much harder time discerning to what extent we have become enmeshed in the world and compromised biblical principles. It has become much more difficult to differentiate what is helpful and edifying from what is unnecessary and harmful to our walk. Pastor Dickau submits, "By naming these idolatries and repenting of them, we are freed to embrace the costly demands of the gospel and to live out of God's restorative power in our lives."[39] Arriving at the point of naming our idols may be a frightful prospect, and one that can be achieved only by the grace we find in Christ. Do we believe this? Do we believe that in fact we gain by doing so, without having to give in to the angst of letting go of the self? This is why unbelievers resist the gospel of transformation and of surrendering to Christ; they wrongly assume that their lives will lose all excitement. "What will it cost me? Will I have to give up all fun in life?" These are questions we frequently hear from seekers faced with making a decision to accept or reject Christ. Alas, many Western Christians are now experiencing the same anxiety when facing the surrender of their idols for obedience to Christ.

Bonhoeffer distinguishes this as a misunderstanding of God's grace in Christ; he states: "Cheap grace is grace without the cross, grace without the living, incarnate Jesus Christ. Costly grace is the gospel. It costs people their lives. It cost the life of God's Son, and nothing can be cheap to us which is costly to God."[40] In putting our choices under God's sovereignty and in relation to the cost that was paid that made grace possible, we will be able to discern and understand what is required of us.

One Regent College scholar suggested that we are quite content to lead our lives apart from God's power. Of course, we pray for His blessings over our work and ministry and for His help; the irony is that "if God shows up, that's okay, but if He doesn't, that's okay too; we'll carry on just the same." This professor's evaluation of our lives is that although we invoke the help of the Almighty, when we do not get an answer or He seems to tarry, we already have set the wheels in motion to find our own solution to the problem. In our Western mind-set, in North America in particular, problem solving is what we do. This means we generally do not even think twice about stopping to ponder another way. For us as Christians, to change this mind-set means taking time to pray over the matter; something that has largely disappeared from our daily lives. This is not to suggest that we do not pray, but rather that we do not set aside time during prayer to truly hear God.

Bonhoeffer maintains that

> if grace is the data for my Christian life, it means that I set out to live the Christian life in the world with all my sins justified *beforehand*. ... I can therefore cling to my bourgeois secular existence, and remain as I was before, but with the added assurance that the grace of God will cover me. It is under the influence of this kind of "grace" that the world has been made "Christian," but at the cost of secularizing the Christian religion as never before.[41]

We must therefore recognize that many of our Christian habits amount to sentimental religious practices and piety, far removed from any reality in Christ.

Gerhard Leibholz, brother-in-law to Dietrich Bonhoeffer, wrote that according to the latter, "all kinds of secular totalitarianism which force man to cast aside his religious and moral obligations to God and subordinate the laws of justice and morality to the State are incompatible with his conception of life."[42]

If we look at the last twenty years of Western Christianity, several secular laws that counter divine principles have crept into our society. While some of these laws were meant to eliminate discrimination and inequality, putting these laws into practice has, in actual fact, gone beyond their intent, to the detriment of other groups of people, such as Christians. For example, political correctness has developed a life of its own to the point of absurdity. As an example, because of the religious connotation of the word *Easter*, a school in Seattle forbade students from referring to Easter eggs as such and required students to call them "spheres." The school inadvertently did Christians a service; Easter eggs and bunnies are of pagan origin and symbolize rites of fertility. This widespread practice is far from Christian; hence, it is ironic that this school and other Seattle governmental organizations showed concern for the "religious" connotation. It does, nevertheless, show how insidious humanists are in their pursuit to eradicate from society any wording that might have any perceived religious undertone. While we might shrug in annoyance at such foolishness, other more important events have troubling repercussions on Christians in society. When Christian high holidays became challenged by the politically correct, Christians did not oppose the majority acceptance, at least not in a way that would be heard, and today we keep quiet lest we are mocked or, worse, face criminal charges. We have forgotten what it entails to be followers of Christ. We feel shame and embarrassment, and while we may internally cringe at the injustice of it all, we nonetheless have slowly adopted this situation as normal.

Paul Roy submits, "If you are recognizable as a countersign to the established order, you have to expect that the established order will begin to be uncomfortable with your presence and activities." We must ask ourselves, are we recognizable as countersigns? Can the secular world see a difference in our comportment, in the living out of our faith? Are we pious, practicing sentimental religion that moralizes without transforming deep within? If we are, then it is the bold facing up to our weakness that is required. We must stand up for what we believe as Western Christians and for all of God's creatures regardless of their position and religious or nonreligious stance.

Rather than slavish legalistic adherence to denominational beliefs and practices, it is an outward-reaching action and proclamation of our faith through a transformed and consecrated life that cares for others, as did Christ. Bonhoeffer asserts: "When we are called to follow Christ, we are summoned to an exclusive attachment to his person. The grace of his call bursts all the bonds of legalism."[43] The opening quote from Acts at the beginning of this chapter demonstrates the decisive action the new believers took in bringing all the idolatrous paraphernalia to be burned in public; this was not a quiet, hidden event.

From experience, the hardest part of following Christ and living out kingdom principles is in breaking the habits and comforts that have taken hold of our hearts. This difficulty is not so much due to general indifference, but more so because of the idols that have taken residence in our hearts and mind. Goudzwaard suggests that

> Living out of messianic hope . . . requires that we leave our protective shelters behind and put our future, our prosperity and if necessary our whole life in jeopardy for the sake of truth and justice. ... Our acts can be a call for the mobilization of the forces of God's kingdom in a time of doom, just as Esther's act was centuries ago. ... We must break publicly with those *means* in which we have put our faith, and we must distance ourselves from those *goals* which define the meaning of life for us. These goals and means form barriers to practical obedience and to genuine non-ideological loves.[44]

The sinful dependence on the self, often disguised by pious expressions of reliance on God, belies whom we are serving. Without admission of such deep-seated individualism that mocks our true reliance, we cannot move forward; there is no way around it. Clearly there is no painless solution, no easy fix. The difficulty of discerning and breaking this conundrum is compounded by self-gratifying Western societies, which regularly reinforce that we can achieve anything we want, any way we want it. The tragedy is that the same mantras have assaulted many of our churches and fellow believers. How can we distinguish the real from the counterfeit if this deceptive self-actualization is offered as something good? To be sure, not all self-actualization is wrong or bad but when refined in the fire of truth, how much will remain as valuable?

The battle therefore is not only against our habits tainted by secular values but also against the false piety inside our churches and among Christian circles. Keyes warns that the latter two are more difficult to conquer, since challenging those self-serving values will attract not only criticism but also vehement opposition.[45]

The ultimate moral challenge from God is at a deeper level than being good and kind. This is the ultimate moral challenge—that hope rests in complete and excuse-free dependence on God and His forgiving grace, plus nothing. This forgiveness is joyfully offered to us through Christ.

Our being "Christian" does not depend on how nice and friendly we are, but on how genuine we are. This becomes a thorny issue, since so much of our identity is tied up with platitudes of being nice and polite. We love to be loved; consequently, we become too afraid of speaking out and thus appear to have little backbone. This may sound insensitive, but think about it: how often do we keep our peace for fear of offending, of saying the wrong thing? It is too easy to hide true feelings and opinions behind a wall of politeness. As Christians we must ask ourselves: "Is my being polite a form of dishonesty? How often have I unwittingly used this so that I don't have to confront the other?" This too requires repentance, forgiveness, and renewal. How else can we reconcile others to God if we have not faced ourselves truthfully? The joyous outcome of transformation and reconciliation, however, will benefit Christians and non-Christians alike.

Newbegin asserts: "Before the cross of Jesus there are no innocent parties. His cross is not *for* some and *against* others. It is the place where all the guilty are forgiven."[46] We therefore all stand before him as guilty, yet with the incredible realization that in Christ we have been forgiven; unmerited and unconditionally, forgiven. We cannot possess the slightest sense of superiority over any non-Christian; it is pure grace that grants us pardon.

Making a Break with the Status Quo, Moving towards Action

Once we act upon the conviction for the need to change, we are assured that we can count on the help of the Holy Spirit. Jesus said that

He would not leave us orphaned. In the idolatries previously identified, technology, consumerism and entertainment played a big part in keeping us comfortable in the status quo. With God's grace we can move into action. It is fair to say that this will require perseverance in prayer and a desire to please God in order for us to receive the power to act in such a way that our conviction has staying power. Too often we spring into action on our own steam only to fall down and give up a short while later. We must admit to God our total helplessness to change, so that Christ's power can start effecting change in us. Tim Dickau warns us, "When we don't initiate people in the practice of confession and repentance early on, we prevent them from entering into God's transforming power."[47] The transformation happens first in our minds, when we realize our sin. Then in our hearts, where pride makes way to grief and leads us to confession, as we submit our minds and hearts to God. James enjoins us to confess our sins to one another so that we may be (physically) well (James 5:16). Unconfessed sin brings sickness. It did in James's time, and it is no different in our time.

In Romans 12:2 (ESV), Paul commands us to "not be conformed to this world, but [to] be transformed by the renewal of your mind, that by testing you may discern what is the will of God, what is good and acceptable and perfect." The renewal of our minds is possible only through the Holy Spirit. Since we are exhorted not to be conformed to this world, but to be renewed in our minds, we know that praying for such renewal meets with God's will and is therefore granted.

Turning Away from Our Idols

It is in the privacy of our homes, where we do what we want and decide how we should do it, that idols have found their way into our lives. In contrast, in a community-based social structure, it is nearly impossible to escape accountability, which may also safeguard individuals from falling into temptation. However, we prize our individualism so highly that any challenge to it is seen as an offence to our very freedom. But is it really freedom? Or does individualism bring enslavement to those things we cannot battle on our own? How can we reach out and extend God's reconciliation to others if we are unable to *un*entangle our own net of deceit? Author and theologian Michael Battle, in suggesting reconciliation for the world, offers

What those of us who want to be reconciling individuals must do is resist the allure of individualistic thinking. In a very real way, getting out from behind the television or computer screen and having dinner with the family or going to play tennis with a friend is a step toward our becoming reconciling persons. We need to place reasonable boundaries around our individual desires and to seek to create a society and a church that looks out for the good of the whole. We need to engage in activities that ask more of us than do television and computer games. If television is the focal point in our lives and we never ask more of ourselves than the effort required to watch television, we won't be able to develop the skills we need to become reconcilers.[48]

Individualism keeps us from consulting others when making decisions that might be uncomfortable. For instance, it is ironic that when faced with a serious medical intervention, we long for the reassurance of loved ones and friends, and even ask their opinion. Yet when it comes to spiritual decisions and concomitant spiritual surgery, the tendency is to sort it out alone, often for fear that others may point out glaring issues that need to be surrendered to God's rule and sovereignty: issues we may not be ready to abandon. We would rather not have others tell us what to do and prefer our own counsel, justifying our course of action, much like an addict who deceives herself or himself that smoking less will eventually lead to total cessation.

Unfortunately, such methods do not work, as long as we try to solve the idolatrous addiction alone. Renouncing to shut ourselves off would be a first step to finding support and solidarity in overcoming our idol(s). God gave us the gift of community so that we could help one another.

To restore our role as reconcilers, becoming salt and light once again, requires rediscovering and relearning those skills that will break down barriers of self-imposed isolation. That rediscovery will allow us to re-engage the world of family and community to cooperate with God in proclaiming His kingdom. "The personal choices that we make about our lifestyle also have an effect on society. ...The world is looking for people whose lifestyles makes them recognizable as Christians," says Paul Roy[49]. So, how can we get started? Let's look at some options.

Entering His Presence—God's Desire to Restore Us

With King David we cry out to God, "Against you, you only, have I sinned and done what is evil in your sight" (Psalm 51:4, ESV). David is fully aware that God sees him in secret, even when nobody else is witness to his actions. Sin against self, our neighbour and our family is ultimately sin against God. When David acknowledges his sins and the fact that he was born in sin, he entreats God to give him a new heart, to cleanse him and wash him, and to restore the joy of his salvation (verses 7, 10, 12). David knows only too well that he cannot generate any of these things in his own strength, and that only God can bring renewal and restoration. This, then, is our hope, that no matter how deep our sin and guilt, it is not beyond God's help and desire to restore us. Even when we are not fully aware of how our sin affects God and others, we must understand that confession to God and to one another is of crucial importance. Just as in Jesus's ministry, confession, repentance and turning away from sin is an ongoing call, so we too must look at confession and repentance as something that we undertake as a matter of course. Tim Dickau explains how this became an integral part of his church's worship: "the movement of worship, the confession of our idolatries and sin, along with a concomitant confession of God's mercy, has consistently been woven into all of our worship services … confession and repentance are now embraced as foundational practices in the Christian life."[50] Such practices will begin to bring healing in ourselves and by extension in our Christian family communities, our places of worship, and our places of play.

Taking Stock

Temptation and sin will be with us for as long as we live in these mortal bodies. No amount of good intentions, discipline, or remonstrations will help us conquer sin. Our only victory lies in Christ, who conquered sin on the cross. For many of us the fact that we hear of God's divine love for His creatures so often without experiencing its reality makes us unsure of its depth. We have lost the wonder and mystery of Christ's power over death and sin. At the risk of sounding banal, this is our only hope, truth, and path to real salvation. Tragically, we have lost a sense of outrage towards the Enemy. Unless we proclaim in righteous anger, "Christ is victor"[51] and the powers of evil have no hold, no place, and no right in our lives, we are merely mouthing that Christ is victor while our hearts remain cold, our minds counter in doubt, and our lives testify our unbelief.

What to do? How do we fall in love with God all over again? Maybe truly for the first time if we have not before? Faith and love are gifts of God. When we pray for these gifts, which by their very nature are God's will and pleasing to Him, we must entreat the Almighty until we receive those gifts.

George Mueller, a great nineteenth-century man of faith, received everything at the hand of God in prayer. He said that God's children do not receive because they do not persevere in prayer until they have obtained their petitions from God; they give up too soon.

I would suggest that giving up too soon is not necessarily a result of impatience, although it could be a factor, but is more due to a lack of conviction that God truly hears us, especially if a pernicious sin still embattles our lives. "How can I expect God to answer my prayer if I'm still overcome by lustful thoughts?" or "Surely God isn't hearing me because I'm still giving in to dishonesty." We can each fill in whatever refrain is relevant to us. But that's just it, isn't it? If each of us could attain God's favour through victory over sin achieved by acts of sheer will and discipline, why, then, would God have bothered sending Jesus? If we thought we could slay sin and cast it forever out of our lives under our own power, would we not be replacing one idol with another: the idol of self-satisfaction and of personal achievement? Paul emphatically told the Ephesians that they were saved by grace alone and not by their own works, so that no one could boast.

This of course does not imply a passive acceptance of "Well, that's just the way I am," but an active reliance on Christ with the unshakeable trust that He will see us through in our time of need (Hebrews 4:16).

Newbegin reminds us how Jesus stated that it is harder for a rich man to enter the kingdom of God than for a camel to go through the eye of a needle. Even Peter felt a moment of despair when he uttered: "Then who can be saved?" to which Jesus replied, "With men it is impossible, but with God all things are possible." Newbegin opines, "The fear is lest I should put my trust in anything other than God's grace in Jesus Christ; the confidence is in the infinite abundance of his grace to me and to every one of his creatures."[52] Until the truth of God's grace becomes part of our breathing, of our waking and sleeping hours, we will continue to attempt to overcome sin on our own. This will inevitably lead to doubt, failure, and giving up altogether. Just as getting up and getting dressed is second nature, so should be walking in God's grace and in its freedom. Let us be clear that this is God's grace that demands our heart, mind and will. It is not a cheap grace of the "once saved always saved" variety—which falsely allows us to go through life without spiritual responsibility.

When we inhabit God's grace it follows that our love for God will be kindled and will grow. Until we fully grasp what grace is—what His love means—you and I will continue to walk blindly and stumble in our sin.

"Show me, Lord!" was my cry when I came to the crossroads of faith as a twenty-four-year-old. "Show me who you are! Whether you exist, or whether you are man's own making." He did show me, through the Holy Scriptures. I keep encouraging people, believers, seekers and sceptics alike to ask God, who will unfailingly answer. This is His desire, that we should know Him, not just for our own selfish desires such as salvation and liberation from troubles, but so that we may know Him, fall in love with Him, and as a result seek to please Him and honour Him. "God, what is your pleasure?" as opposed to "God, this is what I'd like" will propel us nearer to Him, so that we in turn can sense His pleasure in us.

The sheer impossibility of succeeding on our own makes running into Jesus' arms that much easier. The single most liberating experience that I had when meeting God on His terms was the epiphany that I did not have to prove anything to Him. He loved me and accepted me just as I was. The deep insecurities and feeling of worthlessness and the useless attempts at trying to please a demanding and never-approving earthly father was nothing that God had neither witnessed nor was unaware of. There was no need to pretend to be someone else; there was no need to get God's attention and favour by trying hard to do and say the "right" things. All those life-robbing chains fell when Christ affirmed my personhood and inestimable worth in the loving eyes of a heavenly Father: "for I did not come to judge the world but to save the world" (John 12:47b, NASB). Yet there were later times of spiritual darkness and disobedience that made me doubt the constancy of God's love and forgiveness. It is only as His words reminded me that because of such moments Christ had to die, that I dared to continue the journey in His presence. His desire is for the reconciliation of humankind to God.

Proverbs 24:16 (NIV) tells us "for though a righteous man falls seven times, he rises again," and Jesus reminded His listeners, "Those who are well have no need of a physician, but those who are sick; I came not to call the righteous, but sinners" (Mark 2:17, RSV). Regardless of what secret idols we discover, and regardless of where we are when we take stock, the insurmountable can be made surmountable by the healer of spirit, body, and mind, "Christ is victor!"

There Is No Room for God and for My Idol(s)

We may be lured into believing that we are only dabbling in the things that clamour for our attention, and that idols are harmless; that is a patent lie the Enemy tries to ensnare us with.

The truth of the matter is that we are really created to give our heart and attention to the One who created us. The pace of our contemporary culture and work environments has created more and more stress with a need to accomplish many things simultaneously, and consequently we are exhausted. This is not by divine design. It stands in the way of our being able to hold God as our single-minded affection. Jesus does not give us a way out; He said: "'You shall love the Lord your God with all your heart, and with all your soul, and with all your mind.' This is the greatest and first commandment. And a second is like it: 'You shall love your neighbour as yourself.' On these two commandments hang all the law and the prophets" (Matthew 22:37–40, NRSV).

Love, as God created it, is so powerful that it brings all other aspects of life into perspective. It respects and honours our family members, our employers and co-workers, our Christian brothers and sisters, *and* our enemies. Love gives us the divine power to achieve a balance that no surrogate can accomplish; it helps us to act in ways that would otherwise be humanly impossible. Whatever the idol(s) that stands between us and our affection for God, His all-encompassing love can unhook us and redirect us to Him. Jesus, when hearing the petition of a father with a convulsing deaf-mute son, said: "Everything is possible for him who believes." It is interesting to read the reaction of the father: "And immediately the father of the child cried out, and said with tears, Lord, I believe; help my unbelief" (Mark 9:23–24, KJV 2000). The father wanted to believe with all his heart and did believe that Jesus could heal his son. At the same time there was inner doubt—the kind of doubt that often resides deep in our subconscious and we do not dare acknowledge. It may come as no surprise that when we are struggling, be it with one idol or several idols, we inwardly groan with a sense of powerlessness. We forget that He who overcame sin and death is one and the same. If only we would realize how utterly impossible it is for us to overcome our idols on our own! It is only Christ who can; He is trustworthy even when we are not. A desire to overcome and the perseverance in prayer to break free from our idols meets with God's will and will not go unanswered. We must stand fast and refuse any suggestion from the Enemy that our prayers and outcries will be all for naught. "Christ is victor!"

Disappointment with God

There is a disconnect between our daily life and our spiritual life. Although many of us pray for help and guidance, too often there is no clear answer to our silent petitions and outcries. A deeper prayer life suffers at the hand of family and work pressures, and downtime is used to "chill" and "veg out," with little energy left for prayer. God is no longer an integral part of the moment-by-moment events in our daily lives, and as a result we have a low expectation of His active interventions.

Maybe we have an unspoken hesitation about whether God really hears us. Our corporate prayers are all too often spoken with the lips while the heart does not truly believe that they will be answered. "After all," we may reason, "many petitions have gone unanswered. It is all well and good for those grand prayer warriors and for the first church, but in our day-to-day does God really hear?" Even in times where we have offered fervent prayers to God, believing His biblical promises, lack of answered prayers gradually strains and erodes our relationship with God. Yet, regardless of these instances, Jesus said, "Truly, truly, I say to you, whoever believes in me will also do the works that I do; and greater works than these will he do, because I am going to the Father" (John 14:12, ESV). So, what has gone wrong? "Did I not pray fervently enough? Long enough? Loud enough?" I would submit that it is not so much our individual guilt as it is our lack of obedience as the body of Christ.

Probably foremost is our lack of love for one another, followed by our lack of unity. The very thing Jesus prayed in John 17 was that our love for one another and our unity would be a sign to the world that God sent Jesus indeed and loved the world as He loved Jesus (John 17:20–23). In some way we believe that our religious gatherings and programs suffice, that revival is just around the corner. Perhaps we have been blinded by the assumption that we are well, when in fact we should be buying healing ointment from the One (Revelation 3:18) who promised that streams of living water would flow out of our hearts (John 7:38).

Some of us have experienced disappointments when we felt that our prayers for transformation have gone unanswered. "I have tried and tried, and prayed and prayed but couldn't change. I have given up. I guess God wants me to be this way" are words I hear from believers who have genuinely called out to God. Yet we are reminded that God promises to hear those prayers that conform to His will. Transformation to become more like Christ is in God's purview. If such is the case, it may be a lack of accountability that reinforces and affirms our willingness to allow God to transform us. Prayer to God and at the same time an unwillingness to be accountable will prove counterproductive. Perhaps we need to enlist the help of trusted others when we are seeking to break a sinful habit through prayer. While we pray for deliverance of an idol holding us captive, we must seek the strength and witness of a buddy to stay on course. Even the apostles did not minister in isolation, which should empower us to look for someone to come alongside and struggle with us, lest we become either irreparably discouraged or conceited. We must be reminded that the Trinity operates in community and not in isolation; we are not designed to go solo, so how can we expect to conquer adversity by being segregated? It is not possible, contrary to what the world would like us to believe.

God's compassion for the repentant heart resonates with the psalmist, who sings: "Nevertheless He regarded their distress when He heard their cry. For their sake He remembered his covenant, and showed compassion according to the abundance of his steadfast love" (Psalm 106:44–45, NRSV). In Christ we have an unbreakable covenant with God, and we can be assured that God does see our distress and hears our cries. Let's take Him at His word and not become faint-hearted.

When God Seems Silent

Paul says: "[T]o him who by the power at work within us is able to accomplish abundantly far more than all we can ask or imagine, to him be glory in the church and in Christ Jesus to all generations, forever and ever" (Ephesians 3:20–21, NRSV). What power is at work within us? Undoubtedly, if we belong to Christ, it is the Holy Spirit, but how can we see His power truly at work? Unless He works in us, there is no hope; our feeble efforts are worthless and of no consequence. Do we see God's power at work? Do we have that power? If we did, we would certainly see God much more at work in the world and in our communities. Oh, that we would grab hold of that power and see God's mighty work in ourselves and those around us.

At this point we must pause and seriously consider the fact that except for sporadic and clustered answers from God, for the most part He is silent. His silence is deafening. No amount of Bible knowledge, sermons, mouthed prayers and theology will change that; only a general repentance will achieve a turnaround of events. Of course it starts with each one of us, but it is much bigger than each of us; our individualistic thinking prevents us from seeing the bigger picture, to see what God sees, to feel what God feels. Together as brothers and sisters we need to return to God. We experience God's grace, forgiveness, and gracious answers to prayers, but that is not enough! As part of the family of God, when one member suffers, we all suffer (1 Corinthians 12:26); when one part is diseased, we are all contaminated. What do we know of God's sadness? His desire for us? No more and no less than what we can read for ourselves in the Scriptures. We corporately know, deep down, that things cannot carry on as they have to date and that maybe too many of us are living in denial. Admission is the first step on the road to recovery; spiritually it is no different.

I honestly do feel God's sadness in the same way as I feel His pleasure. The former, however, overshadows the latter. How can you and I be satisfied that unbelievers and nominal Christians have not found God? How can we not see there is something amiss when people do not break down and convert to the living God in our church services and in our midst? How can we go to work and return home day after day and ignore people who are spiritually starving, suffering neglect, abuse, and injustice? "Well, that's not my gift," you may say. But that is not the point. It is not that we need to serve independently; as a body of Christ we are to be "full of good works" (2 Corinthians 9:8; James 3:17). I am not talking about salvation here but about love. Truly, only Christ can make this happen, and yet, unless we recommit to love Him as He loves us, we shall remain cold and self-absorbed.

Repenting and returning, individually and corporately, may move God's heart so that He hears us again as He did in Nineveh.

Through His incarnation, Christ opened the way to freedom, not just from sin but also from anything that stood in the way of reconciliation to God. Christ invited humanity to take up His standard and follow Him in a radical way: by living for God, His kingdom and one another, and by building a living church made of living members who proclaim His way of life.

Through His incarnation, Christ provided a sure access to the Father's kingdom. He did not promise a journey free from difficulties, but rather a journey wrought with perils and pitfalls. He did, however, promise that He would never leave us or forsake us (Deuteronomy 31:8; Hebrews 13:5). It is up to us to either accept the challenge or continue a life dedicated to comfort that will not satisfy, a life of unbridled pleasures and secret vices that cannot gratify and only lead to spiritual death, a life dedicated to vain idols that cannot fill us and only rob life.

Trusting in God, beyond what we perceive with our senses and beyond the silence of God, we can find refuge and fulfillment, and reach beyond ourselves towards other people.

To be sure, the journeys will vary from person to person, and none of us can say what will and will not work for each. There are sufficient testimonies that give us glimpses of a God who is at work among us, but there are no ready formulas. Besides, any time believers have tried to bottle God when a move of the Spirit swept among the people, they utterly failed. When they tried to turn His work into a blueprint, it became self-serving. A formulaic attempt to recreate an outpouring of the Holy Spirit takes our focus away from God by unconsciously acting in our own strength. The Holy Spirit will not be held captive.

When Jesus said, "A new commandment I give to you, that you love one another: just as I have loved you, you also are to love one another. By this all people will know that you are my disciples, if you have love for one another" (John 13:34–35, ESV), He was neither just suggesting some impossible action nor pronouncing some esoteric fact. He meant it; it was a command, not an option. Yet we seem to have turned this into a nice saying without consequence; our track record is clear that we fail this command.

But if Jesus knew that we were going to fail at this command, was He wrong to give it? Did He not know that we would falter in our obedience? Not at all. Jesus knew that upon His return to the Father He would not leave us orphaned, because He sent the Holy Spirit. When the Holy Spirit resides in us, we are enabled to love one another and in turn reflect the love of Christ to those outside the household of faith. The command to love one another was not meant as a platitude. We were meant to act on it. Faith must come into play with the knowledge that when Jesus gave us this command, He fully intended for us to keep it. What if we still fail? We have the promise that God will help us along; in Proverbs 24:16a we read: "for the righteous falls seven times and rises again, but the wicked stumble in times of calamity." We can be confident that being righteous in Christ means we will rise up again. If not, we should ask ourselves whether we are truly the Lord's, or whether there is some unconfessed sin that needs to be brought to light preventing the Holy Spirit from living within.

The love of God utterly desires to invade our being so that we can obey Jesus' command. Otherwise, why would God have sacrificed His only Son? As incomprehensible as this love for us is, God has given us unmistakeable proof of our reconciliation to Him in Christ's sacrifice. Satan would have us believe otherwise. It is against Satan that we must speak God's Word and silence him as Jesus demonstrated when He was tempted in the desert. Satan tried to trip up Jesus by misquoting Scripture. To accept defeat is to believe the Enemy and disbelieve God, giving the Enemy the power he no longer holds.

Unforgiveness and Offence

In the past year I have discovered startling instances of having offended certain brothers and sisters, without being at all aware of doing so. In one case this happened with good friends who then grew distant. In another case it pertained to a brother I scarcely knew.

In the first instance, a mutual acquaintance hinted at a situation where I had said something that had a deep impact on their grown children and consequently on these friends. I have no recollection of the offending remark I made, but considering my state of mind at the time, I cannot rule out that such took place in the heat of the moment. What is utterly painful is that six years went by without my knowledge of the situation, or the opportunity to right the wrong.

In the second case, I made a passing remark to a brother, but as I neglected to put the remark into context, it had been received as an offence. It was not until later that I sensed I may have offended him, albeit unintentionally. Upon seeing him again two weeks later, I approached him, and he threw himself away from me in anger.

All of the parties involved were part of the church family, in Christian ministries or in leadership positions; it is unthinkable that we would continue teaching and admonishing others without seeking to confess and reconcile within. How this must hurt our Father, and how this must disappoint our Saviour, who prayed that the all people would know us as His followers by our love for one another (John 13:35, ESV). Thankfully, in both situations reconciliation eventually took place. These examples demonstrate how crucial it is that we keep short accounts towards each other, and that we seek to be candid, whether we're at the receiving end or the source of an offence. As the body of Christ, together we are to be one as the Trinity is one, so that the world would know that God sent Jesus (John 17:20)!

Growing Cold

The preoccupation with lifestyle, comfort, material goods, and entertainment keeps us working at a frenetic pace. Many of the distractions the world offers blinds believers and nonbelievers alike to the temporary nature of life. Those of us who try to stay involved in church activities find that we are exhausted and stressed out. Others amongst us see this and limit themselves to jobs and families, which can be stressful enough without adding church activities. Ultimately, what is the purpose of work and family? What goals do we strive for? Can we, as followers of Christ, have the same goals as those who live outside the faith community?

"For the love of money is a root of all kinds of evil, and in their eagerness to be rich some have wandered away from the faith and pierced themselves with many pains." (1Timothy 6:10, NRSV). This verse has been bandied about often, to the point of turning many off. Yet I have had to ask myself how seriously I should take Jesus, who spoke similarly when He stated: "No one can serve two masters; for a slave will either hate the one and love the other, or be devoted to the one and despise the other. You cannot serve God and wealth" (Matthew 6:24, NRSV). It is a piercing statement when examined more closely. What does God want from us? Our heart, all of it, not just in part; our affection, not in part but complete; our devotion, not divided but undivided. I must confess that my sense of self recoils at this. Of course I love God! Don't you? But fully? Wholly? Surrendering every part of my heart to Him? Do I? Do you? You see, this is exactly the crux of the matter. At some point in life some of us realized the need for Christ's love and forgiveness and surrendered. There were no half measures. The consequent renewal, joy, and rest found in repentance were real. God undeniably welcomes His prodigal sons and daughters back into the fold.

With the passing of time, our love cools (to be sure, this does not describe everyone), and the hard work of staying surrendered takes its toll. Discouragement, self-doubt, condemnation, worldly distractions—you name it—little by little our former love is but a shadow of what it was when we first encountered the living God.

There are many reasons for this estrangement, as it were; lack of discipline, cares of the world, and disappointments, to name just three. These tend to lead us to a point where we go to church out of habit, obligation, or fear of criticism. Although we sing along, clap, and raise our hands, the question is, during the few hours we are in church, are we going through the motions, or are we fully engaged in the Lord with our hearts and minds? Tevye's song from *Fiddler on the Roof* comes to mind: "Tradition … tradition …!"

Maybe in the West we have had too much time on our hands. Our lives, free from persecution and wars experienced by previous generations and other nations, have made us complacent, self-centred, and unwilling to forgo our comforts. They have, in a way, contributed to the present surge in secularism and the decline of Christianity in the West. Historically, where civilizations reached their peak and became amoral, self-serving and undisciplined, ethical and spiritual decline ensued. Similarly, Western Christianity has lost its compass, strength and purpose; it has become sentimental, self-righteous and comfortable.

Nothing, however, forces us to continue down that path. Returning to God, desiring what He desires, entrusting ourselves to Him and allowing Him to once more take the reins and guide us, will assure not only a reawakening among us but also a move to conversion, for those of us who have not yet truly met this life-changing God.

Breaking the Stranglehold: Repenting and Returning to God
Step 1

What better way to reach out to God than by praying His Word to Him! Psalm 51 is a first step to regaining, and gaining for the first time, God's perspective and to walk in the power of the Holy Spirit. When we stand before tasks that appear insurmountable from a human standpoint, praying a Psalm or a Scripture passage that speaks directly to our state of heart and mind will open the way to God's merciful intervention. Those who already practice this have found that it is vital to make it a daily habit until we receive God's answer, and the longed-for breakthrough is received. Something else happens in the process: our inner being becomes at rest, and a slow but certain transformation takes place. At first we may not notice, but then it takes root and the shackles fall away. It may take some time; the point is not to let go until the prayer has taken hold of both the praying person and heaven. Psalm 51 may best convey the prayer of freedom from sin—and idolatry. Meditating on this psalm without hurrying through it will help our hearts to hear the healing voice of God. We must take care to remember that this is a prayer and not a magical formula!

Psalm 51:1–17, ESV
Have mercy on me, O God,
according to your steadfast love;
according to your abundant mercy
blot out my transgressions.
Wash me thoroughly from my iniquity,

and cleanse me from my sin!
For I know my transgressions,
and my sin is ever before me.
Against you, you only, have I sinned
and done what is evil in your sight,
so that you may be justified in your words
and blameless in your judgment.
Behold, I was brought forth in iniquity,
and in sin did my mother conceive me.
Behold, you delight in truth in the inward being,
and you teach me wisdom in the secret heart.
Purge me with hyssop, and I shall be clean;
wash me, and I shall be whiter than snow.
Let me hear joy and gladness;
let the bones that you have broken rejoice.
Hide your face from my sins,
and blot out all my iniquities.
Create in me a clean heart, O God,
and renew a right spirit within me.
Cast me not away from your presence,
and take not your Holy Spirit from me.
Restore to me the joy of your salvation,
and uphold me with a willing spirit.
Then I will teach transgressors your ways,
and sinners will return to you.
Deliver me from bloodguiltiness, O God,
O God of my salvation,
and my tongue will sing aloud of your righteousness.
O Lord, open my lips,
and my mouth will declare your praise.
For you will not delight in sacrifice, or I would give it;
you will not be pleased with a burnt offering.
The sacrifices of God are a broken spirit;
a broken and contrite heart, O God, you will not despise.

Step 2

Pastor Dickau suggests that

> Through the practice of confession, we come to recognize
> and name—before God and one another—some of the
> robust forces that misshape our lives and society. Through
> the practice of repentance, we turn away from these forces,
> towards a merciful God, trusting in the power of the Holy
> Spirit to transform us and escort us toward new life in
> Christ.[53]

God says He is a jealous God—why? Because He knows that false
gods destroy us to our very core as God-created beings. They harm us,
making us spiritually and morally barren. False gods make promises that
only turn to ash in our mouths and, in the end, make us less human.
Their deception is our demise; they turn us into utterly selfish and cruel
creatures, unable to feel love, compassion, and care for others—the exact
opposite of the divine, liberating, and life-giving gift of God. Only God
can satisfy and make us whole. His jealousy is *for* our good and *against*
the counterfeiters; He desires our well-being and wants to protect us from
those fraudulent idols that cannot give eternal life. As with all aspects of
our lives, He will not interfere but respects the freedom of choice He gave
us; hence, the stronger is His jealousy of the human-made idols that want
to deceive and entrap us.

Unless we stop and take a ruthless and courageous inventory of our
lives before God and confess, we cannot move forward. Therefore, the
practice of confession in Pastor Dickau's church is sound and key to
repenting and returning to God. It is unfortunate that in our Protestant/
evangelical traditions we have moved away from confessing our sins. Since
confession has become a private affair between God and me, there is little
accountability to the church family. In this respect, believers in the Roman
Catholic church who hold to this sacrament are at an advantage. While I
am aware of its imperfections—especially when people go to confession
without intending to change their ways—I am also cognizant that many
go filled with contrition and a real desire for change from the sinfulness
that besets them.

Among healing ministries, the practice of disclosure and confession is an indispensable step to receiving healing. Outside of these ministries the habit of public confession is rarely found. Only in recent years have churches like Pastor Dickau's reintroduced and integrated confession into their services.

It is as if we have forgotten that this praxis is very scriptural. James counselled believers to "confess your sins to one another, and pray for one another" (James 5:16, NRSV). Paul urges the Corinthians to restore a brother to fellowship through forgiveness when he had confessed his sin of immorality and subsequently repented thereof (2 Corinthians 2:5–8). Paul goes so far as to state that if they forgive any repenting brother, so will he (verse 9)! The reason for this forgiveness: "so that we may not be outwitted by Satan; for we are not ignorant of his designs" (verse 11, NRSV) or "lest Satan should take advantage of us; for we are not ignorant of his devices." (NKJV). Confession and forgiveness are powerful tools against the Enemy. Satan knows that if he can keep us from confessing to one another and from forgiving one another, he gains an advantage over us, he outwits us, and we become weak, sickly and ineffective Christians. It makes sense, then, that this confessing to one another follows our confession to God in Psalm 51.

Confession therefore is a crucial step to experiencing transformation and renewal and helps to effectively eradicate the sin of idolatry and any other sin from our midst.

Step 3

We must acknowledge that unless God in His mercy chooses otherwise, healing will take time, and we will stumble until Christ has wrought His complete healing into the fragments and idolatrous parts of our hearts and lives. Nevertheless, God promises that He will never leave us or forsake us (Hebrews 13:5), and that when doubts assail us we can look up to the cross and know that He will take those moments and failures upon Himself—even, and especially, when we do not feel His presence in that moment.

Having worked through the most pernicious strongholds in our lives, we can move forward in our renewal.

Questions
1. Which areas in my life have I identified as bringing dishonour to God?
2. In what ways am I showing indifference to God, taking Him for granted?
3. Which idolatrous attitudes and activities do I need to confess, repent from and surrender to God?
4. Do I need to confess being lukewarm and lacking in love?

Prayer

God, in Christ you have declared me your (son/daughter) so that I may call you Father.

Forgive my indifference and lack of love. Thank You for not giving up on me and for continuing to woo me. Fill me with the gift of Your love so that I can once again stand in awe of You, overflowing with love. Father, only by truly loving You am I able to love my neighbour as I should, and in a way that is pleasing to You.

Grant me grace, in Christ's power, to set aside my prejudices. I desire for Your Holy Spirit to renew my mind to conform to Your will.

Eduardo's Story

I grew up in the west side of San José, Costa Rica. I came to Canada when I was twenty-six, in 2008, because I had heard of Regent College in Vancouver, and about its integrative approach to faith, the marketplace and life in all its dimensions.

I grew up as a nominal Catholic, with an awareness of God. And halfway through high school several things happened:

When I studied microbiology I was amazed at the intricacies and level of perfection in which cells operate, and how perfectly the body is tuned up.

Two people I met and befriended impressed me with the radiance that emanated from their faces. Somehow, I knew that this was because of Christ in their lives.

I also experienced a personal crisis in my late teens. I was sad with my life. For about four months, and without anyone inviting me, I attended a Catholic church service in my home town. I kept asking God to intervene and to help me. About a year later I was invited to a non-Catholic Bible study where the leader shared a very formulaic explanation of the gospel. Being very rationally minded, as I am, the "economic transaction" of the sacrifice of Christ made complete sense. While I may not fully subscribe to such a method of explanation today, in God's providence He used this to bring me to faith. I was twenty at that time.

After this experience I started attending an evangelical nondenominational church. I also joined Bible studies and an organization called Unidos por Cristo—a parachurch group that sought to bring evangelicals and Catholics together. There my walk of faith became one of personal piety and sanctification, but with hardly any implications for the social dimensions of life. Most evangelical Christians in Costa Rica are very focused on individual salvation and personal prosperity; on conversion at the expense of a shared discipleship; and on conversion at the expense of living as a people. Even where the call for discipleship exists, there is not a strong sense of walking in the Spirit as the family of God— the renewed Israel. In most cases this often remains at the level of lip service. For example, I remember the posture of one of the pastors leading a Bible teaching session. Being a wealthy man, and living in one of the best parts of the city, he stated that he didn't bring people into his house. This represented one of many inconsistencies between the individual and social understanding of what the gospel is actually about. It is one of many instances of how we have a tendency not to lead by our lived lives.

I would dare to affirm that most evangelical Christians don't engage much with economics, politics, the media, or education—at least not from a Christian perspective. We basically construe our Christianity upon the secular Western assumptions of present-day politics, economics, etc. and thus leave the autonomous principalities and powers unchallenged and unchanged. For reasons too elaborate to enumerate here, we perceive public life outside the scope of Christ's redemptive activity. (If one engages such things, one is quickly labeled a Marxist; but shopping malls and multinational corporations are seen as the bringers of peace and prosperity, and many Christians participate in them wholeheartedly. The *pax americana* has certainly taken over.)

This poses a perplexing paradox. On a theoretical level we agree that Christ is Lord, but on the practical level we leave such structures largely unredeemed. As evidence of that, in my eight years of active involvement in evangelical Christian circles, I don't remember a single time that a Bible study or sermon was ever preached regarding wider issues that transcend the life of the individual. The gospel is mostly—if not solely—reduced to personal and interpersonal psychology: it is a therapeutic gospel. So, say, for instance, when we read the story of Moses and Pharaoh, we reduce it to the personal and don't read it as the clash of Yahweh with the false god of Egypt. The question then is asked in the "application" section of the sermon: "Who is *your* Pharaoh?" The Pharaohs are always—*and only*—personal Pharaohs: mere problems that need to be addressed in the life of the individual, in an individual way.

By the grace of God, we recognize that every human bears the divine image. Because he or she was created by Christ, and is loved redemptively by Christ, that alone gives human beings immense bestowed worth. But biblically understood, Christ is the origin and destiny of all things, not only of individual people—he is "the ruler of the kings of the earth" (Revelation 1:5). The Spirit is the life-giver and sustainer who leads us into the fullness of God's purposes in Christ. All of life should be touched by the gospel. Living out one's faith only a couple of hours in church on Sunday but ignoring every other aspect of daily life—such as in choosing the products one buys, opting for public versus private transportation, dressing in ethically made clothes, and so on—that is an embarrassment to the biblical testimony.

My humble estimation is that Christians in Vancouver, Canada (where I have lived for the past five years), are exceedingly concerned with not making other people uncomfortable. In their well-intentioned politeness, they are often "too nice." It is tricky to make judgments, but on a general level if I were to compare churches here with those in Costa Rica, it may not be an exaggeration to say that Vancouverite Christians are not passionate about the gospel in all its glorious fullness. In a sense, there is a sort of numbing apathy towards Christ. However, compared with my native country (where we are heirs of a degraded evangelicalism brought about by American missionaries, and where we have thus truncated the gospel to a message of personal therapy), I would dare to say that although Costa Rican evangelicals are more alive to the Spirit of God, we do lack some of the biblical foundations that Canadian Christians often have. Surely both churches have much to learn from each other.

This is important to tackle, because such politeness can easily lead to apathy, which in turn leads to indifference. Regent College and the people within it have been profoundly formative for me, and I will always be deeply grateful for my time there. That said, knowing that Regent's mandate is to foster life-engaging discipleship, I have been deeply surprised by how the college, being as it is at a secular university campus, is doing little at an institutional level to engage the assumptions and worldview of the university in which it is placed. (There are, of course, reasons for this: the horrors of the residential schools being one of them. But in my short time at Regent, there was not any sort of sustained effort of dialogue or engagement between UBC and Regent professors, challenging and learning from each other.) There seems to be a huge gulf between the two institutions, when there could actually be intelligent, loving, and respectful cross-feeding. One thus wonders if by being politically correct we may actually be embracing the muddled relativism of the culture—which is nothing but yet another subtle form of ideological imperialism. It would be good to move on from that towards a respectful pluralism (which is not the same as relativism) and cease to be ashamed of the gospel—as Lesslie Newbegin often summoned the Western church to do. In the end, we are called to be loving and faithful to God, not relevant and polite to our neighbours (although there's nothing necessarily wrong with the latter). When we seek to be relevant, we often compromise the uniqueness of the Jesus Christ. But back then as he is now, the crucified and risen Lord is and will remain a stumbling block for many. Lest we domesticate into another of the many deities of the postmodern pantheon, may we proclaim His glorious deeds—in fear and trembling, with joy and boldness.

CHAPTER 7

Standing Firm—
Resisting Evil—Loving God

Resist him, standing firm in the faith, because you know that
the family of believers throughout the world is undergoing the
same kind of sufferings.—1 Peter 5:9, NIV

od, how can I love you better and act on the inner impulses to serve
and obey you? Many, if not most of us, have deep longings to be
closer to God, as attested by the plethora of books on hearing
God. At times it seems to be a barrier that cannot be defeated: "The spirit
is willing but the flesh is weak" (Matthew 26:41). We may feel pumped
after a particular sermon, retreat, or emotional appeal from the pulpit,
only to slip back into the routine and demands of everyday life. Why does
the energy we feel when we hear God speak to us vanish the moment we
resume daily life?

Maybe we are approaching it from the wrong perspective. In the
Christian evangelical tradition in particular, there is an expectation and a
pressure that we must "go and tell the world and make disciples of Christ."
Instead, how about truly being "little children"? It may be easier for those
of us with children to imagine; but our own childhood recollections may
help too. Regardless of whether our childhood experiences were positive
or negative, there would have been an innate trust in mom and dad. What
mom and dad said was accepted unequivocally. Having mom's comforting
words after we fell or felt sad, feeling dad's strong grip when crossing the

street or performing a difficult task, all implied trust: "Mom loves me." "Dad's going to take care of me." Any early memories reflect moments of abandon and trust that all would be well. Isn't it harder as adults, though? After all, we are supposed to show strength, resiliency and control— especially when we do not always feel in control. Naturally, two cannot be in control at the same time, so it is either going to be God or me. All too often it is me. *Help!*

For the longest time I would get quite upset when well-intentioned people would say, "Let it go," or "Let go and let God." What exactly is that supposed to mean? What is letting go? How can we trust God so completely as to be concerned only with Him and the others He cares about? Forgetting ourselves and allowing Him to provide His guidance, solace and strength, so that our lives can weather the storms?

Depending on our temperament and life experiences, we may only see a slow and probably painstaking process of change in our lives. In a society of instant gratification and constant reminders that there are remedies to cure us instantly from our pain, the thought of a long and perhaps arduous process is not at all appealing. Yet when we reach out to God as trusting children, He promises that He hears us; those calls become prayers immersed in His will. "Abba, hold my hand while I cross this valley" invites the loving care of our heavenly Father as much as it would our earthly one.

Loving God

Can we remember a time when we could not stand being away, not even for a moment, from our sweetheart, so intense was our love? Now, can we imagine what that would be like in regard to our Creator? The One who gave up His crown and throne to live among us and pay the ultimate price because of His love for us? How come we, in our progressive civilization, have lost sight of that and became ho-hum in the face of such consuming love, meeting it with profound indifference?

Sometimes I think we are no different than the citizens of ancient Rome who clamoured for *panem et circenses* (bread and games) and could not care less about the blood spilled in the arena as Christians were torn apart by wild animals. Just so long as the audience had "fun." Being so preoccupied and distracted by our idols, we have developed spiritual

ADHD. No sooner have we left that inspiring sermon, book, or Christian event than we turn back to our idols and find ourselves trapped again. Yet deep down we hunger for transforming change and genuine closeness to God. Wait! Did God not promise that He would give us a new heart (Ezekiel 11:19; 36:26)? That if we repented, He would turn His face back to us? Hear us? (2 Chronicles 7:14). God even goes so far as stating, "Before they call I will answer; while they are yet speaking I will hear" (Isaiah 65:24, ESV). God already knows our unspoken longing for realness with Him. When we receive that gift of hearing and hear His voice, we in turn can help others hear also.

We must, at all cost, move away from being lukewarm towards God. Jesus gave us a warning in Revelation that He would rather have us be hot or cold. He cannot bear those who are lukewarm; it is an insult, and Christ tells us that He spews out those who are (Revelation 3:15–16). Consequently, we cannot and must not sit on the fence. We must earnestly ask the Lord for that new heart, for that transformation, until we are totally suffused and imbued with His love and warmth. In turn we will radiate His love and warmth to others. We must not allow the Enemy to leave us with the mistaken notion that if we behave "Christianly," attend church, and participate in Christian programs, then all is well. This deception prevents us from dying to the self and living for Him. By God's grace, and according to His promises, we can prevail and allow Jesus to set us once again—or for the first time—on fire. Oh, that we would each desire this love with all our heart and being and taste the blessings and love of the Lord.

Our lack of faith keeps us from taking up the promises of God so that we can overcome our idols. Without faith we cannot see God's power shape our lives and those of others. Jesus refers to this in the Gospel of Mark: "Jesus said to them, 'Only in his hometown, among his relatives and in his own house is a prophet without honour'" (Mark 6:4–6, NIV1984). Jesus could not perform any miracles there, except lay his hands on a few sick people and heal them. And *he was amazed* at their lack of faith. It struck me how Jesus' power could not be manifested because of the unbelief of the people and relatives in his town. The text states that he was astonished at their unbelief. I personally think this reflects our own unbelief on frequent occasions. The good news is that we do not have to live there any longer!

We can move towards God in faith and allow Jesus to bring healing from our idolatrous attachments.

Step 1
Standing firm in our resolve to conquer idols

It is at this point that the list of offenses, idols, and other hindrances exposed earlier will assist us in making a full confession. To stand firm in our resolve to overcome the idols by God's grace, we must resist the temptations and justifications the Enemy will put before us, such as: "I'm in full control of my technology; I need it for work, to stay in touch in case someone needs me." I enjoy this reality show; it helps me understand how people live; how not to raise my children." James exhorts us to "resist" and that the Enemy *shall* flee from us (James 4:7). I believe our dilemma comes from being unable to wait on the Lord to act.

As revealed earlier, it can take months, even years, before the Lord answers; after all, it is "in His time." We can agree that this is little consolation when an answer is needed *now*! I have come to understand that often the silence in response to my prayers seems to be directly related to my lack and oversight of something I needed to repent for. Repentance however means serious business. We need to be aware that adopting a casual attitude of, "God knows", towards unrepented sin demonstrates a fundamental lack of understanding about the seriousness of sin. True repentance and a changed heart follow deep, heartfelt regret and contrition. We would only be fooling ourselves, because God knows our hearts, which is why we cannot fool Him. "A broken and contrite heart oh God you will not despise" (Psalm 51:17b, ESV). Not "maybe," not "when I think you're worth it," none of these; a genuine brokenness suffices in God's eyes.

Here is a good moment to take our lists and, on our knees, confess each of the idolatrous offences while prayerfully asking the Holy Spirit to reveal other transgressions to us. It is not something we should rush, although we may be tempted to do so. For some of us this may be no more than an exercise of the will, and that is okay. The key is that we humble ourselves before God and submit to His sovereignty; the release should follow despite our feeling doubtful or undeserving.

Through confession and repentance we have been given a clean slate; we are now free to enter God's presence with boldness and expectation. To be more like Jesus meets God's will; to pray for salvation of loved ones is according to God's will; to pray to live as a witness for Him in our work, actions, and ethics is in keeping with God's will. When our hearts are in tune with God's will, we can and must expect a favourable reply. If we keep short accounts with God and by faith accept His forgiveness according to His promises, we know He hears us. Nevertheless, let us not think the Enemy will not interject, attempt to block, interfere and above all sow doubt and fatigue. At this stage we must stand firm, refusing doubts that may assail us or the fear and unbelief that may hamper our prayers. "Jesus is victor!" Let's keep standing on that truth. Let's not give the Enemy any room to distract us. He has *no* power; he has *no* room in a believer's life unless we allow him.

Step 2
Standing firm in and through God's Word

"Evangelically rooted churches can so easily slip into forming biblically literate people and stop there, rather than forming disciples of Christ."[54] We must become true disciples—that is, followers of Christ in every sense of the word, living transformed lives. Not in a moralistic, way such as "Thou shalt not lie" (which we have historically excelled at), but rather transformed by and for the love of God. In the same way that couples in a loving relationship are willing to do those things they do not particularly care for but do them anyway, because they are moved by their mutual love. When we love there is no room for moralizing, but instead there is room for respect, joy, and willing sacrifice.

Often we think that knowledge of certain Scriptures and pious outward platitudes are adequate to satisfy our Christian obligation. Religiosity, however, is not a proof of faith and of true devotion to God. Unless we allow Christ to circumcise our hearts and let Him flow freely through us, we shall fail miserably at entering into a genuine and intimate relationship with Christ. Jesus showed contempt for hypocrisy; quoting the prophet Isaiah, he stated: "These people draw near to Me with their mouth, And honour Me with their lips, But their heart is far from Me. And in vain they worship Me, Teaching as doctrines the commandments of men" (Matthew 15:8–9, NKJV). We should be watchful that we do not hold on to our traditions and rituals at the expense of God's principles.

In Zechariah, God spoke through the prophet of His disgust and weariness with the people's worship and prayers. He wanted and still wants broken and humble hearts; hearts ready to love Him and be loved in return. Such a bond stands strong and cannot be broken; it will withstand any Enemy endeavour and prolonged harassment. Paul, in his closing remarks, said: "Be watchful, stand firm in the faith, act like men, be strong. Let all that you do be done in love" (1 Corinthians 16:13–14, ESV). "Christ is victor!" We must completely grasp this, and we will thus be enabled to hold fast.

Step 3
Systematically resisting our idols

Dr. Dickau states that "we are confronted with the same choice that the people of Israel faced in the desert: will we worship God, or will we worship idols?"[55]

To resist our idols may require countercultural actions and attitudes, such as the following examples.

Resisting Consumerism

In the areas where the idols of consumption allure, accumulating and consuming can be reversed. As Tim Dickau shares: "As an act of resistance to the idolatry of personal wealth, many people in our community are choosing to share vehicles in order to free up money and time devoted to maintenance, or to give vehicle access to those who couldn't afford it. … Resisting the accumulation of private wealth will also bring us into conflict with powerful market forces."[56]

In an age where many churches promote prosperity and encourage believers to seek wealth as a sign of God's blessing, the deliberate choice of doing with less will go against the grain of both our possessions-crazed society and Christians who have become trapped in the snare of unsuspectingly serving Mammon. Choosing moderation and simplicity without forgoing quality and durability, we model a different way of life that allows time for relationships rather than for things at the expense of people.

In the New Testament, Christ heralded a new paradigm, one of servanthood and a walk in inner beauty and simplicity, not in wealth.

Resisting Overwork

The demands of accumulation and consumption have a propensity to create bondage to work, not necessarily because we enjoy the work but because working more affords us those things. This chase for material wealth is usually at the expense of family, friends, and faith community. As Dr. Dickau explains, "paid work often tends toward the extremes of over or underemployment."[57] In his church community some people have opted to work less and to form home communities with others "in order to participate more in kingdom ventures within the church and neighbourhood … each of us had to resist the temptation to submerge ourselves in our work and thus fail to embrace the other life-giving aspects of the creation mandate."[58] Resisting overwork will restore family values by prioritizing what is important and thus have a positive impact on society.

Resisting and Redeeming Technology

In our present day, this area is probably one of the most difficult to resist, because of its sheer prevalence in all aspects of our lives. God's power and grace must be implored until the unhealthy hold breaks to make room for a guarded and healthy use of our technology. Someone or something can exert power over us only in the measure that we allow it access to our hearts and minds. We may falter and, through God's grace, get up repeatedly until He has so captured our hearts and minds that these inanimate objects can no longer imprison us.

Resisting of course is active; there is no opportunity for passive mental acknowledgement, which would only deceive us. For instance, I can decide to leave my cell phone at home on Sunday—at least during the short time I'm involved in worshipping God and listening to His Word. It will produce healing in our relationships, starting with God and flowing to others in our lives.

By changing the paradigm of how we approach our Sabbath (Sunday or other focal day of rest unto the Lord), in regard to technology, the Enemy is forced to retreat in defeat. Unless the Enemy is defeated, we will experience unrelenting harassment. We must therefore resist technological idols. Jesus knows only too well the idolatrous lies that keep us captive, in bondage, and without hope. In God's liberty we can find the grace and guidance to use technology in a way that is redemptive and countercultural and that honours God.

Taking the steadfast position that, thanks to Christ, the idolatrous minions *are* defeated will close the door to unhealthy technological attachments. Resist therefore we must, in the power of Christ and of God's Holy Spirit. "Christ is victor!"

Resisting by Practicing Reconciliation

According to theologian Michael Battle:

> We need to learn to place reasonable boundaries around our individual desires and to seek to create a society and a church that looks out for the good of the whole. We need to engage in activities that ask more of us than do television and computer games. If television is the focal point in our lives and we never ask more of ourselves than the effort required to watch television, we won't be able to develop the skills we need to become reconcilers.[59]

When we allow the Holy Spirit to harness our hearts and minds, and our focus turns away from the self to God, and by extension to the well-being of the others, a renewing shift will start to take place. The pull of the self in its fear for self-preservation will not disappear overnight. The habitual indulgences of our secret and not-so-secret wishes, applauded by society, will fight with all their might against the thought of having to give up the smallest amount of time and effort for the pursuit of God and our neighbour.

The freedom to pursue God as the best choice for ourselves and our neighbour is what God proclaims throughout Scriptures and what Christ models in the New Testament. It is the Holy Spirit who convicts us, and it is Christ who is able to set us free from our self, and rend asunder the idolatrous tendencies. This hunger within us, which we have been stilling with all things temporal, alienates us from the highest friendship: friendship with God. He desires to satisfy us. God longs to have us as partners to bring His kingdom to others so that they too can be free. He waits for us to let Him transform us.

Step 4
Living for others

As we actively resist the Enemy and the temptation of pursuing our own desires and relief from hardships, we grow to be more outward-looking, as God desires. Dr. Dickau suggests, "As we seek justice for the least as a church, we will need to provide an ecclesiology that empowers us to dialogue about justice issues in a way that leads to action, even if we don't all agree."[60] A desire to see justice and compassion, concern for others and a focus away from the self is the natural outcome of a life in the process of transformation.

In our individualistic environment, where living for the self is applauded, it has become very difficult to discern what living for others entails. Many may well say that their friends on Facebook, for instance, are their community. Social network communities may be experienced as real communities for those who interact within them; nevertheless, it is not exactly the community God has in mind. Jesus moved among and interacted with those who were on the margins of society. Because we often connect with or like people with similar interests or agendas, it is hard to find marginal groups within a social network, let alone interact with anyone who is on the fringe of our personal circles, online or off. This requires an about-face for each of us, and reaching beyond our comfort zone to those we would normally not interact with, for the sake of God's kingdom. If we all remain cloistered in our existing social circles, how then can God's forgiveness, reconciliation and love be proclaimed? Our actions, more than words, need to reflect that we belong to a different kingdom; our citizenship is not from here, we are only temporary residents in our present domain.

To make our divine citizenship real for others will require a fresh understanding of whom we belong to. In today's global sphere, it is easier for people to grasp. Immigrants often have a better appreciation for this. Although they might have become citizens of their new country on paper, many still carry their homeland in their hearts. As Christians we may appreciate the good things our earthly citizenship offers. At the same time our hearts should be burning with love and longing for the kingdom to which we belong. In caring for others, as tokens of God's grace for his creation, we demonstrate visible expressions of God's kingdom among us.

To live for others will require an understanding of their circumstances but also, more importantly, of how God sees them and what, in obedience, our role should be in loving them and giving up our comforts for them and the sake of God's kingdom.

****

As we are all created with unique traits and personalities, each of us will need to approach the steps in a way that is most effective and ask the Lord to show what works best for each unique situation. I have discovered that without exception, God has directed me to what was best, sometimes through trial and error, sometimes through an inner assurance, and sometimes through books that invariably open my understanding. Such assurances and directions were, and still are, typically followed by a deep sense of serenity instead of struggle and indecision.

Providentially, there are no how-to manuals or fix-it guides, as these would be contrary to a relational God. Often we may find God's direction in conversation with a trusted friend or family member. God will surely guide any of us who desire to please Him and do His will, in tune with our personalities.

What if I don't hear Him? This deafness may require further examination. Too many people have lost touch with themselves. To protect ourselves from pain or disappointment, we tend to cut off our emotions and compartmentalize our lives; consequently, we are no longer able to hear with the heart. We need to allow Jesus to bring healing to our hurt and wounded selves and renew His identity within us. In recognizing our real identity in Christ, created according to God's image to love God and others, we can once again, through His healing, become capable of immense compassion and care for others.

His Promises
- ❖ If we return to Him, He will hear us.
- ❖ He will give us a new heart.
- ❖ He will make us and all things new.
- ❖ He will never leave us or forsake us.
- ❖ He will help us overcome the Enemy.
- ❖ He will not leave us orphaned but send us the Holy Spirit.

He Has Not *Promised Us*
- ❖ a life of ease (according to the New Testament paradigm)
- ❖ a life free of temptations
- ❖ a life free of suffering
- ❖ a life of wealth
- ❖ a life of health
- ❖ a life free from persecution

Christ said: "If the world hates you, know that it has hated me before it hated you" (John 15:18, ESV), "and you will be hated by all for my name's sake. But the one who endures to the end will be saved" (Matthew 10:22); "I have said these things to you, that in me you may have peace. In the world *you will* have tribulation. *But take heart; I have overcome the world*" (John 16:33, ESV; emphasis mine).

We can and must, by His grace and according to His finished work, overcome the Enemy and see through his tactics. As the time for Jesus' return grows ever nearer, the Enemy is working overtime to keep people from entering God's kingdom and Christians from being effective. Satan very much desires for us to be asleep and captive to our idols.

Lord, we want to be set free from shackles that keep us from loving and serving You. If we believe, we *shall* inherit: "The one who conquers will have this heritage, and I will be his God and he will be my son [or daughter]" (Revelation 21:7, ESV). On the other hand, should we remain in denial and persist in our present state, according to God's Word, we shall not prevail.

Do we believe Him? Can we trust Him? Do we care? With all of the aforementioned promises, we should be encouraged, knowing that Christ already overcame *for* us! The apostle Paul exhorts us to not grow weary doing good and to resist evil. Let us, as the prodigal son did, run back to our heavenly Father, who awaits us with open arms and has promised us a new heart!

Questions
1. Which areas in my life are more vulnerable and prone to fall back into idolatry, and need more protection, in order to stand my ground for God?

2. What are some Scripture passages that can encourage me to stay the course?

3. What Scripture verses can I meditate on daily (at work, when going to work, school, etc.) that focus on God's love for me, and express my love for Him in return?

4. How can I learn to live and love those outside my circle as Jesus taught? What Scripture passage can help my mind to refocus and be renewed to conform to God's command to "love one another as I have loved you"?

5. I can pray those Scripture passages aloud every day. [If too many, then rotate them and use two verses at a time.]

Prayer

My heavenly Father, I am powerless without You; powerless to overcome my sinful and idolatrous nature. Fill me with Your grace and power, so that I may love You so completely that my sinful habits will no longer take the place that is rightfully Yours.

As You forgive me, grant me the grace to forgive myself and others. Should I have wronged others, grant me the courage to ask their forgiveness and make amends.

CHAPTER 8

Proclamation by Example— Kingdom Values

Reconcilation isn't a pill we can take; it's a process we have to learn. The most basic elements of this process of reconciliation are: contrition, confession, repentance, and ... reconciliation.—Michael Battle

As Michael Battle states, reconciliation is a process, not an overnight experience. We should be patient with ourselves as we work through this. In a sense, it is an operation: we allow Christ to excise that which is harmful to ourselves and others, and which stands in the way of an intimate relatioship with our heavenly Father.

Contrition

There is no reconciliation without contrition; a feeling of sadness and heartfelt remorse for all we have allowed to come between God and us. Contrition is not feeling sorry for ourselves; it means that we are truly sorry for having hurt God, and our neighbour by extension.

Confession

We acknowledge and admit that we offended God through our sin. With contrite hearts, we ask the Holy Spirit to bring to our recollection the idols that had taken up residence in our hearts. We also ask the Holy

Spirit to bring to remembrance any other wrongdoing committed against God and our neighbour, family, member(s), or others.

Repentance

Repentance follows contrition. With remorse for our having ignored God's loving call to obedience, we now repent. In Christ's power, we turn away from the idols that had temporary power over us, and we turn back to God and His life-giving grace, ready to obey and follow Him unconditionally. Repentance requires a conscious renounciation of our former idolatry, to, once again, embrace God's ways, in the assurance that Christ's strength will empower us to obey.

Reconciliation

God's mercy towards us is renewed, even if we sinned while we were already His children. Forgiveness, because of Christ's redemptive sacrifice on the cross, is always available. This is the infinite grace of God, often incomprehensible to our human thinking. Having turned back to God, He awaits us with open arms, as the father did in the prodigal son's return.

God rejoices that we have forsaken that which leads to spiritual death, and He welcomes us back. In Christ we are reconciled once again to the Father.

As we go through the process of reconciliation and consequent renewal, we are freed from the shackles and the hold that the idols exerted on us. In this newfound freedom we can rejoice before God and move forward to live out our faith in everyday life.

God's Love, Our Loves

Seeing ourselves as God sees us within the human story makes it easier to understand our role in God's kingdom and how we are to be before God and our neighbour. Here, *neighbour* is not understood as other believers, but rather as those who, like us, inhabit God's creation. It is hubris to believe that once saved we belong to God's exclusive club and that somehow we have become better than others.

"How can we be truly loving and not just tolerant? How can we be freed from cultural notions of nicety and embrace biblical notions of sacrificial, covenant compassion?"[61] asks Tim Dickau. Indeed, how are we to make that transition? Especially in the case of polite Christians, for whom the notion of being nice and polite is so deeply ingrained in the fabric of the larger society, moving to the next stage of embracing all of God's creatures, irrespective of their beliefs, in a way that represents Christ is not an easy process. For most of Western Christian society, however, moving from a self-centered and tribal way of life (as in church tribe, the family tribe), may require a relearning of what sacrificial living means. We have been so pampered by ease and selfish pursuits and the access to a life of instant gratification that all this instantness has made it nigh impossible to practice patient, thoughtful waiting, and even going without, for the benefit of humankind. Christlike loving, then, will necessitate a renewing of our mind and a spiritual mind-set that will expunge the selfish longings that scream for our attention. Loving God—falling in love with God—is the only way to excise those egotistical demons and to love others in a way that is pleasing to Him and represents God in our present world. It is absolutely possible! It is absolutely attainable and it will not be an instantaneous fix! It will take time. How long? That depends on the level of disconnect from one's inner being—the God-created being not the selfish destructive being. Many of us in Western society have lost touch with our true person and have learned to hide genuine emotions in order to live according to the expectations of others. The heart and the mind have become disconnected and therefore it takes more time to hear the voice of God and be healed from this duality and fractured self.

Through God's promise to Abraham, Israel was supposed to become a great nation and a blessing to all nations (Genesis 12:2). By extension, being grafted into Israel's tree through Jesus, we too are meant to be a blessing. In the twenty-first century it is essential we find ways of cooperating with God, by fulfilling the task He places upon us, one which may be different for each of us. Such obedience to God's calling brings meaning and hope to our world—by example more than by our words. In other words, we may want to hold our tongues and live out God's Word so that we inspire people to want to know this God incarnate.

Our Faith Community First—A Community of Unity

Paul Roy suggests, "Very often, the vibrancy of the Christian community depends on our ability to recognize and respect the uniqueness of each person's call from the Lord. We must learn to hear our own names, and to help our brothers and sisters to hear theirs."[62] In hearing our name called out by God, we move beyond our ethnocentricity to being children of God irrespective of our tribal affiliation and by so doing, we encourage others to hear their call also.

We look to Christ once again, the first great equalizer who already bridged the generational, cultural, and economic divide for us: "There is neither Jew nor Greek, there is neither slave nor free, there is no male and female, for you are all one in Christ Jesus" (Galatians 3:28, ESV).

Tim Dickau suggests that "by belonging to a community that values common practices such as hospitality, service, justice seeking, prayer and contemplation, we are empowered to turn away from these idolatries and give our lives to living in right relationship with God, one another, our neighbors, ourselves, and the whole of creation."[63] By means of sharing and celebrating our otherness so that we come to experience a oneness, we close the gap that otherwise keeps us divided.

Moreover, if we take Dietrich Bonhoeffer's statement to heart, to live "a life of uncompromising adherence to the Sermon on the Mount,"[64] we will in fact arrive at seeing one another as unique and valuable creatures of God. We will no longer see that which keeps us separate and aloof; instead, we shall discover that which makes us similar and unites us to one another and to God. In finding our common ground in Christ, we join forces to announce and further God's kingdom to a nonbelieving world and at the same time affirm our unity to one another. At times we may find it challenging to embrace one another; our love for Christ will spur us on beyond our limitations. In turn, the love of Christ will drive us to maintain the course that not only honours Him but ultimately makes us an active part of the greater good, as God intended.

A Community of Justice

Over the centuries people have striven to fit God into a human understanding, into their respective communion and denominational rigidity or liberality. Our church history is mottled with blood and crimes perpetrated in God's name. Unfortunately, these crimes are still being committed today in various parts of the world when people take a stand for Christ. Institutionalized religions or other world religions react by condemning such conviction as blasphemous or criminal; it is as if hell unleashes all its fury on the follower of Christ.

As the time for the Enemy shortens, pressure mounts and the ferocity to create maximum destruction escalates. Whether under the form of outright religious persecution in regions where one cannot openly be Christian or under the guise of political correctness, justification for violence, be it physical or psychological, cannot be tolerated. As our lives unfold in a new light and are allowed to be imbued with Christ's gospel, we are no longer content to sit back and let world events slide with indifference. Paul Roy explains that

> We Christians must project justice in everything we do. Our faith must be one that, of necessity, celebrates humanity as the place where divinity dwells. It must be a faith that is intolerant of the destruction of human life, of the denigration of human dignity, of the breaking of the human spirit. Our faith must lead us to openly oppose injustice, oppression, and discrimination of any kind. Our faith must be the kind that moves the world from violence to gentleness, from selfishness and greed to generosity and sharing, from hatred to love, from sin to holiness.[65]

Such revolutionary principles may seem unattainable, and so they would be were it not for Christ, who achieved a resounding victory through His death and resurrection. Through His incarnation He heralded a new era, decreed an eternal kingdom, and dealt a decisive blow to the Enemy.

Honouring God, Honouring Our Neighbour

As the time for the Enemy shortens, it is time for us to be aware and awake. One of the ways we can bring defeat to Satan is by honouring God and, by extension, our neighbour. From a concern for the other's salvation to a commitment to proclaiming God's kingdom through Christ, our efforts must be filled with respect for those who don't share our beliefs. We take the time to listen to the other first. Sometimes we have to keep silent and simply be there to offer solace and encouragement by both our silence and our undivided attention. Only after giving the other our time can we expect the other to grant us equal time and earnestly listen to us.

Proclaiming Salvation and Reconciliation

Newbegin, in looking at the matter of salvation, asks

> What is the meaning and goal of this common human story in which we are all Christians and other, participants? ... [The Christian] tells it simply as one who has been chosen and called by God to be part of the company which is entrusted with the story. It is not her business to convert the others. She will indeed—out of love for them—long that they may come to share the joy that she knows and pray that they may indeed do so. But it is only the Holy Spirit who can so touch the hearts and consciences of others that they are brought to accept the story as true and put their trust in Jesus. ... [Salvation] is inclusive in the sense that it refuses to limit the saving grace of God to the members of the Christian Church, but it rejects the inclusivism which regards the non-Christian religions as vehicles of salvation ... "the Christian mission must be an affair of love, not an affair of truth" [Citing *Tell Us Our Names*, Orbis Books, 1984, p. 114]. But it is not love which encourages people to believe a lie. ... It is not true that all roads lead to the top of the same mountain. In Christ we have been shown the road. We cannot treat that knowledge as a private matter for ourselves. It concerns the whole human family.[66]

Tim Dickau states, "Salvation does not refer to personal conversion alone, but rather describes God's redeeming work in Christ to restore the whole world—indeed, the whole of creation—to Shalom."[67] We do need to get over this fascination with salvation only, as if Jesus did not have a larger work in mind—the entire kingdom of God.

Salvation implies an element of reconciliation:

➤ reconciliation between the self and God, as God calls us
➤ reconciliation of others to God, as we tell the story
➤ reconciliation of one towards the other in a broken world, as Christ enjoins us to do: "Blessed are the peacemakers" (Matthew 5:9)

If we wish to live out Christ's reconciliation with God, we will need to live counter-culturally. In a world where getting even, or cutting contact, with those who wronged us is the norm, extending wholehearted reconciliation goes against human nature. Such unconditional action will bring people closer together and may open the way to seeing Christ in us, even effect faith in Him.

Michael Battle suggests, If we can love the other, those of other cultures, other nations, even other worldviews, we will open ourselves to the higher reality that we are all children of God. Why reconciliation? The answer is simple: Because it makes us God's children—related to God.[68]

To reconcile others to God and to one another must become as instinctive as breathing. Being immersed in a spirit of reconciliation—by the very fact that we have been reconciled—will inevitably rub off on those around us. When situations arise that threaten unity and harmony, whether in the home, the workplace, among members of the family of God or in the larger global context, a spirit of reconciliation will defuse the hostile occurrences. These events will only become opportunities to live out gospel reconciliation and allow glimpses of God's kingdom.

Proclaiming the Kingdom of God

When the apostle Paul said that we are ambassadors of Christ (2 Corinthians 5:20), his listeners knew that such a position carried the highest responsibility. As we know, an ambassador represents his or her country and is an example of its values, systems and traditions. Through ambassadors it is possible to have access to information, commerce and even citizenship of those countries they represent. What an incredible honour and privilege, then, to be ambassadors of Christ! What a weighty responsibility to live out His kingdom values! This alone should encourage us and ignite our passion for God's kingdom.

Being ambassadors of the Most High implies that we are thoroughly familiar with our Sovereign, His kingdom, and His values. Proclaiming the kingdom of God comprises the values of the Sermon on the Mount; it incorporates Christ's redemptive work for all. Dickau reminds us, "Salvation does not refer to personal salvation alone, but rather describes God's redeeming work in Christ to restore the whole world—indeed, the whole of creation—to Shalom."[69]

Kingdom values are expounded in the Beatitudes.

And [Jesus] opened his mouth and taught them, saying:

Blessed are the poor in spirit, for theirs is the kingdom of heaven.

Blessed are those who mourn, for they shall be comforted.

Blessed are the meek, for they shall inherit the earth.

Blessed are those who hunger and thirst for righteousness, for they shall be satisfied.

Blessed are the merciful, for they shall receive mercy.

Blessed are the pure in heart, for they shall see God.

Blessed are the peacemakers, for they shall be called sons of God.

Blessed are those who are persecuted for righteousness' sake, for theirs is the kingdom of heaven.

Blessed are you when others revile you and persecute you and utter all kinds of evil against you falsely on my account.

Rejoice and be glad, for your reward is great in heaven, for so they persecuted the prophets who were before you. (Matthew 5:2–12, ESV)

Verse 3—A Christian Community of Simplicity

We desire simplicity. Through Isaiah, God says, "But this is the one to whom I will look: he who is humble and contrite in spirit and trembles at my word" (Isaiah 66:2, ESV). A poor spirit is a spirit of humility and reverence. Taking it a step further, it will keep us from focusing on what has no lasting value. In submitting to God's spirit and sovereignty, secular pursuits become insignificant and no longer hold us captive. We are content with living with less and giving more. We are content in the situation in which God placed us. Our desires no longer concentrate on wanting more. The power they exerted over us is broken, and we are free to love our neighbour.

We rejoice that this pleases our heavenly Father.

Verse 4—A Christian Community of Mourning

When we love God through Christ, His Spirit cuts to the core of our being for those things that sadden Him and fill Him with outrage: our sins, sins of others, offences against one another. We mourn the loss of innocence.

In 1 Corinthians 1:7 (ESV) Paul says that "godly grief produces a repentance that leads to salvation without regret, whereas worldly grief produces death." We mourn over our sinfulness, our brokenness, our selfishness, our lack of concern for God's creatures. This kind of mourning is redemptive. Weeping over earthly benefits we might have to forgo brings only spiritual death and sickness. We disentangle ourselves from the unhealthy pursuits of this world and no longer grieve over idols, because we have exorcised them from our midst.

We rejoice that this pleases our heavenly Father.

Verse 5—A Christian Community of Meekness

The Merriam-Webster online dictionary defines meekness as "enduring injury with patience and without resentment." It also means humility, modesty and absence of arrogance. It is important that we mirror those attitudes in a world that has become increasingly loud, arrogant and completely devoid of modesty. As a Christian community we humble ourselves before our mighty God, considering others as better than ourselves (Philippians 2:3), and particularly within the body of Christ.

In Philippians (2:3–5, ESVUK) Paul encourages, "Do nothing from rivalry or conceit, but in humility count others more significant than yourselves. Let each of you look not only to his own interests, but also to the interests of others. Have this mind among yourselves, which is yours in Christ Jesus."

Looking out for the interests of others as well as our own is countercultural. Paul tells us we can have this mind-set because it belongs to us in Christ. By our meekness we invite others to do the same. By not retaliating and by fleeing pride, we participate in God's kingdom. Notice Paul does not insinuate that we cannot at all pursue our interests; it is the manner of pursuit that either sets us apart as children of God or makes us merge with the secular world.

We rejoice that this pleases our heavenly Father.

Verse 6—A Christian Community That Hungers and Thirsts for Righteousness

We hunger and thirst for God—this is our primary instinct. When we hunger and thirst for God, we also hunger and thirst for that which is right. We eschew anything that can bind and oppress others. Whether it is through the work we do or through the investments we make, we should be aware of the implications of our participation. Am I unwittingly involved in labour practices that oppress people and violate their basic human rights—which are also divinely appointed rights? Have I unwittingly invested in companies that perpetuate injustices in countries where human freedoms are being trampled on? Where young children are coerced into labour? As God's ambassadors we operate in righteousness and promote the same in others.

We rejoice that this pleases our heavenly Father.

Verse 7—A Christian Community of Mercy

As God has shown us mercy, and does so on a daily basis, so we in turn must show mercy to others. Whether they deserve it is not our concern; we leave this to God. He alone will judge rightly when the time comes. Our concern should be that we are beyond reproach and exercise compassion and goodness to those who are being mistreated and unjustly oppressed. We should show compassion to those we interact with. If we have been wronged, what is it to us? We bless and give favour, because Jesus commands us to "be merciful, even as your Father is merciful" (Luke 7:36, ESV); it is not an option! So if God forgave me, I forgive, lest God not forgive me; since God showed mercy, I show mercy also; since God showed compassion, I show compassion as well. By this the world will know that we are followers of Christ and that our kingdom is not of this world. By this the world will know there is another standard by which one can live by; one that brings hope and life instead of death and destruction.

We rejoice that this pleases our heavenly Father.

Verse 8—A Christian Community That Is Pure in Heart

Jesus said: "Let the little children come to me and do not hinder them, for to such belongs the kingdom of heaven." It is that childlike innocence that should be present in our lives, in our hearts and minds, and with which we should trust Christ.

In a world where deceit and dishonesty is applauded, our actions and activities are refined in the fire of God's holiness.

In a world where purity has disappeared and immorality is rampant, it is a challenge to be pure in heart. All our activities and thoughts should be pure and reflect the purity of the One whose disciples we are. If this is not yet the case, we should ask God for His cleansing so that our innermost motives become pure and thus infect our actions with virtue.

Dr. Henry Schorr, Senior Pastor at Centre Street Church in Calgary, preaching on the Sermon on the Mount, stated that if we have our thoughts on Jesus, there is no room for impurity. It does not help to refrain from sinning alone; if so, our focus remains on the wrong thing, and we shall surely fall. We should focus instead on "whatever is true, whatever is honorable, whatever is just, whatever is pure, whatever is lovely, whatever is commendable, if there is any excellence, if there is anything worthy of praise, think about these things … practice these things, and the God of peace will be with you" (Philippians 4:8–9, ESV). It is quite impossible to concentrate on temptation when wholly contemplating Christ and His message; on God's Word.

Paul exhorts us: "*If* then you have been raised with Christ, *seek* the things that are above, where Christ is, seated at the right hand of God. *Set* your minds on things that are above, not on things that are on earth. For you *have* died, and your life is *hidden with* Christ *in* God" (Colossians 3:13, ESV; emphases mine). Have we been raised with Christ? Have we died to live for Christ? Is our life hidden with Christ in God? If so, we will be able to carry out what God has commanded us to do. God promises that His peace will be ours. We can know that deep within God shelters and strengthens us so that we may accomplish His will. We rediscover what it is to be childlike, not childish, our lives abandoned to God's care, seeking to please Him and enjoy Him, just as a child would.

We rejoice that this pleases our heavenly Father.

Verse 9—A Christian Community of Peacemakers

This is probably one of God's more difficult directives. Our whole world is permeated with violence. We are visually bombarded by it; our plays are soaked in it; our television shows overflow with it; our mouths are full of it; our lives are held in bondage to it. We attach so much importance to it that we are proud of our military, that we encourage wars and even actively voice our approval—especially in North America. We know that until we reach the shores of New Jerusalem, there shall be violence. What has made us such a culture of violence? To be sure, it is our fallen and sinful nature, but more importantly it is our turning away from God and His precepts, and from obedience to Him, preventing us from seeking peace and reconciliation. How can we possibly break these cycles of violence? Where it depends on us, we are to run away from any form of violence. There is no option; more and more we must embrace becoming agents of peace. Peacemakers are often labeled pacifists, but that is a misinterpretation of what it really means. Pacifism is a secular philosophy that implies passivity. Peacemaking, however, is anything but passive. It is an active form of resistance. Peacemakers offer peaceful solutions when violence seems to be the only way. Merriam-Webster defines a peacemaker as "one who makes peace especially by reconciling parties at variance."

Some Christians disagree with pacifism, citing numerous Scripture passages that seem to justify violence. Even the eschatological allegory in Revelation 19:11–15, describing Christ's return to make war with a sword coming out of His mouth, would seem to suggest a penchant for violence. But we typically pull these passages out of context to suit our arguments. In the Gospels, Jesus did not come to judgde but to save (Luke 19:10; John 3:17). In Revelation, Christ's second coming is to judge, as the time of grace and salvation has come to an end.

In the Beatitudes Jesus is not teaching about the final battle but expounding how we, His followers, should act on a daily basis. We cannot ignore this momentous passage of the Beatitudes, penned by both Matthew

and Luke. Paul, in Romans 12:18 (ESV) advises us, "If possible, so far as it depends on you, live peaceably with all."
We rejoice that this pleases our heavenly Father.

Verse 10—A Christian Community Persecuted Because of Righteousness
What is righteousness? Is it not the adhering to moral and religious laws? Is it not something that is morally right and fair? Therefore, when we see someone being mistreated or dehumanized, does it not make us indignant? And by speaking out against such injustice, does it not put us at risk of being ridiculed, and of being shunned and isolated?

Conversely, when we choose to live according to God's standards, we become unafraid to swim against the standards of a dissolute society, and we expect to be reviled, mocked and humiliated. As a Christian community we are prepared to be countercultural and engage those around us in a way of life that is whole and fosters inner peace. This desperate world is crying out for meaning, for wholeness, and for what is morally good.
We rejoice that this pleases our heavenly Father.

Verse 11—A Christian Community Persecuted and Reviled Because of Jesus
This is not about waving the Christian flag with an air of superiority in an "us versus them" attitude. Because we are followers of Jesus, this is more about making unpopular choices at work, in social settings, and at home; not with the approach that signals "I'm better than you"; rather, it's undertaken with a stand that is thoughtful, deliberate, and compassionate.

Showing our colours is usually tied to social issues and societal mores. We have not really thought hard about the matter of political correctness and how it is affecting all aspects of our lives. How, by simply stating an opinion, we could be labelled racist. By offending someone—and it seems we are always offending someone at some point—we could be accused of committing a criminal offence under the law (a hate crime, for instance). Such nonsensical attitudes to anyone's views removes our freedom of speech. Such bigotry limits even a minister or priest from guiding his or her flock on social issues in accordance to biblical principles. That views from the pulpit or from a politician, or from you and me, become subject to legal prosecution should very much concern us. We need therefore to be prepared and not surprised should we face unjust treatment and persecution because we choose to follow Christ and stand for God-proclaimed values; we celebrate and embrace suffering for His sake.

We rejoice that this pleases our heavenly Father.

Verse 12—A Christian Community That Rejoices in Persecution

Although the New Testament is packed with examples of suffering for Christ, and the rejoicing in that suffering, the notion is so far removed from our Western reality that it begs understanding. We have read the verses, and we sing about it in hymns and worship songs, but embracing suffering for the Beatitudes defies earthly logic. Most of us cannot relate. And yet, we are enjoined to rejoice, to rejoice when people "utter all kinds of evil against you *falsely on my account*" (verse 11; emphasis mine), because we choose not to bear false witness or remain silent when someone is being mistreated. Jesus adds that for us as Christians persecution is no different today than for the prophets in biblical times. We should be joyous in knowing that our "reward in heaven [will] be great"! Alas, we are so myopic in living for the here and now that we find it difficult to comprehend the divine benefits in some future, unseen realm.

Owing to our worldview and the secular mantra for instant gratification, it is tough to grasp this image. We need to pray for comprehension so that we may indeed discern what was penned in the letter to the Hebrews: "For here we have no lasting city, but we seek the city that is to come" (Hebrews: 13:14, ESV). Sacrificing an immediate pleasure for a future gain has become so foreign to us that the concept of longing for this new city remains abstract, except in the songs we sing. When endured for Christ's sake, our adversities are met with gladness, as we are aware that it is only for a time.

We rejoice that this pleases our heavenly Father.

Taking a Stand in the Face of Hostility and Choosing Faith

We come to the conclusion of our thoughts and at the beginning of our renewed journey with God.

We talk about global warming; about the grave environmental dangers of pollution. Now, when it is almost too late, our governments spring into action, or at least attempt to do so. As Christians we must see the invasion and unrelenting assaults of society's machinery as the pollution of our minds and hearts. If many are taking up the environmental cause for the sake of future generations, ought we not to do the same and so much more for our spiritual well-being? We and our children are being spiritually hijacked by idols in disguise; idols that have no mouths to speak and no powers to save. We must decide. We must choose to regenerate our entire being with, and through, Christ and honour the victory He won over sin and death, and therefore over our idols. If we have lost the power of Christ in us and the influence to bring Christ's transforming power to a world on the precipice of physical and spiritual destruction, what hope is left? We must choose faith in Christ in an increasingly hostile and godless society.

If we allow the present state of affairs to continue to go unchecked, we will regrettably be overpowered by the Enemy, and we will be unable to stand when the approaching time of difficulty is fully upon us.

However, by admitting our failings and turning back to God, we will overcome. The ensuing spiritual battle may result in battle scars, and even our lives may hang in the balance, but we will be squarely in God's territory and living out of His strength and grace. One fact is certain: the time is coming when we may have to publicly assert our position *for* or *against* God and will no longer have the luxury of hiding in our private spaces. Imagine if we had the same zeal for our spiritual health as many who faithfully exercise their bodies. Yet in our spiritual lives we have spiritual flab and are incapable of resistance, that is, until we tone those spiritual muscles and become spiritually fit to resist any challenge to our faith. Paul counsels us to take the example of an athlete and run to win the race (1 Corinthians 9:24)—the spiritual race, that is. We may be asked to affirm or deny our beliefs, and unless we start working out at God's spiritual gym, we will be unable to fearlessly declare the One we are loyal to.

What will it be?

"Dear children, keep yourselves from idols" (1 John 5:21, NIV).

Questions

1. In what ways have I been indifferent or oblivious to others, In my immediate family, circle of friends, church family, those outside my sphere of interest?

2. What people groups do I tend to react negatively towards and in a critical, judgmental manner?
3. From whom can I learn when it comes to building bridges of understanding?
4. To what areas in the Sermon of the Mount do I need to pray particular attention?
5. Do I rejoice that walking in my heavenly Father's ways pleases Him?
6. In what ways can I become part of the solution ([for example, in promoting cultural understanding]?

Prayer

Heavenly Father, in Your love for humankind You sent Jesus, so that through His death and resurrection He could reconcile the world to You. Grant me the grace to actively seek to promote Your kingdom by drawing people to You through respect, love, and forgiveness. Help me to be a true ambassador. Amen.

Ana's Story

[Translated from Spanish]

I arrived from Caracas, Venezuela, in 2009 and went to stay with my sister in the south of Spain.

I grew up in a Christian family. Around eight or nine, I could already distinguish between good and bad.

The most important values in my family were unity, respect, and maintaining good communication. For my mother this meant trusting in the Lord before starting anything, and in anything.

We are five siblings: five girls and one boy. I'm the youngest. From my early life I liked music. I was never interested in fiestas or things that the world had to offer. I felt complete in the Lord. He gave me the gift of music, and each time it was my turn to sing at church, I felt very happy and full of love for Him. I never felt like going out in the world to experiment with evil. No, this didn't interest me at all!

From the time I was little, I was always involved in children's worship, and at twelve I had already started to help. It was normal for me to spend time in church.

Why did I go to Spain? After finishing university I worked as a nurse in a hospital. I felt very comfortable and started living a routine that I didn't like in the least. It was as if my life had already ended. I also ran a small dance group. I got up, went to work, went to church, taught dancing, and so the days passed; inside I wished for something more and knew that there was more. I wanted to do something else. ... I think that we are not in this world to follow the way society lives, and if we remain comfortably in our little home, we shall never accomplish anything. Therefore, since I had a sister in Spain, I joined here there. Such was my desire to experience a different lifestyle. In my heart I felt it was what I had to do.

My sister knew a Christian sister who told me about an evangelical church in a nearby village. The first year there was anything but easy. Now that I was in Spain, it was different seeing things from close by than from afar, from Venezuela. It was very difficult here. People, Christians here, have very different personalities. Culturally, they are very shy and therefore appear distant. Not because they don't want to get to know you, it's just that our culture [in South America], although it has the same language, is very dissimilar. In my country when foreigners arrive, we are immediately all over them to make sure they feel at home. One is immediately invited to people's homes to share a meal. My first months in Spain, one or the other came to greet me, but it was not easy to start a friendship.

I loved music; it was hard for me that I couldn't sing at church during worship as I used to in my city. As months went by I started inquiring how I could be part of the worship team, and I had to spend several months being at practice. It seemed it took forever, but the Lord helped me to learn patience; often we desire for things to take place right away but the Lord has his own timing.

One example of how we are different: in my country we hold many outdoor services. In Spain they seldom do, and to be out in the open is also a way that one can evangelize. If you don't go to the people and bring them to church, they won't come. In Venezuela it is very common to have a church service outside on the street so that everyone can hear the good news. The world has much to offer, and we, as Christians, must try to offer many opportunities to listen to the message: use dances, music, and other activities so that as Christians we can bring the message in a distinct way and not just by speech. Here, whatever one does, it's still not enough.

The first year I really felt like leaving and kept asking myself, *What am I doing here?* But little by little I learned about the culture. It was I who had wished to come and learn this new life; therefore, I was the one who needed to get closer to them, and not the other way around. And so it was. I started to get to know people and live among them. I joined the worship team, I got involved with the youth, and one day I even preached and loved it! I was the first young outsider to preach, and I can say that I'm starting to feel at home with my other family.

Culturally, the most notable aspect in Spain is the quality of life, which is very good. It is safe, there is health care for everyone, education, and many other services. On the other hand, there is much freedom to do bad things that don't exist in my country, such as abortion and homosexuality.

As Christians in Spain, like other European countries, we are too laid back in regard to what we do with our time and the priorities we give to things in our lives. For example, it is good that we study the Word of God, but we need to live it as well and share the Word and the life that God gives us with those outside the Christian community. We don't see this as a priority; neither do we build relationships or preach the Word.

I want to encourage people, as children of God, that we live our lives thinking that our Lord is near and that we are His representatives on earth. We are His eyes and need to see what is missing and deal with it the way He sees it. Because we fail to see the way God does, we are like the priest and the Levite in the story of the good Samaritan, and we cross over to the other side. And if there is a taxi, we'll catch it quickly, without looking back!

We're also His hands, and we need to bring them to those who have need, according to his Word, that if we touch the sick in His name, they shall be healed. As a nurse I see the needs daily; there are people close to death and alone, and there is where we should be present.

We are also his feet. We shouldn't go only into the city, where we feel at ease; there are means of transportation to get to where nobody wants to go. For although there are technical advances and a thousand ways that people listen to the message, there are also isolated places Christians need to go to with the message of Christ and where they should remain until most in those places [are able to] keep the teachings that Christ has commanded.

EPILOGUE

A ll the aforementioned, rather than disturb us or cause hand wringing, can serve to rouse us from the somnolence we have fallen into. In realizing the rapid changes that have taken place around us, we can choose to become earnest in relation to the position God has placed us in and in our role as kingdom bearers. We can admit to having succumbed to the idols that surround us and allow Christ to reshape us. We can remain in bondage to our idols and find ourselves overtaken by the Enemy's army, thus denying that Christ overcame him on the cross two thousand years ago. What shall it be? If we had to give an account of our faith right now, what would it be? What would it look like? Would we be able to pass muster, or would we be found wanting? Having fought valiantly in Christ's power to overcome our idols, can we demonstrate God's kingdom among us? In matters of political correctness, would we be able to take a stand for what we believe—even if it meant losing our freedom—or would we accommodate and tell ourselves that we are just being considerate or tolerant of others? Or would we be silent because to speak might incur ridicule? Would we be willing to risk being made fun of by showing whose side we are on without being impetuous, and free from retaliation?

Christ meant what he said, when He said: "Very truly I tell you, whoever believes in me will do the works I have been doing, and they will do even greater things than these, because I am going to the Father. And I will do whatever you ask in my name, so that the Father may be glorified in the Son" (John 14:12–13, NIV). Not seeing these greater works, so that the Father is glorified in Christ, means that something is amiss and that we need to get to the root of the matter. God is not at our service, but we should be at His *and* on His terms, not ours.

Christ's victory over sin and death overcomes disobedience and pride, and any idol in us so that we become gradually more like Him. This is Christ's promise: "See, I am making all things new" (Revelation 21:5, NRSV). Yet as long as we live in this mortal body, sin will be present; we live with this tension. Nevertheless, Christ's presence in us breaks the hold of sin and sets us free to be true light-bearers of His truth. Religiosity, church programs, Bible studies, and Sunday churchgoing can never achieve this. It is a counterfeit of what Christ meant His followers to be: salt and light moved by divine love, compassion, and mercy.

What does it mean, then, for us to be Christian and live out our faith? It is not:

➤ a sentimental notion of Jesus Christ
➤ a belief in an indulgent heavenly father who nods approvingly to whatever we do
➤ sentimental, syrupy music, or frenetic rhythms fashioned after secular music but widely accepted because of a "Christian" music label
➤ a bland following of a Jesus that modern Christianity has transformed into a white, harmless, spineless man, far removed from the revolutionary Christ of the Scriptures.

One common thread among public opinion, including the ones that belong to those who ultimately converted to Christ, is that our Christian behaviour has an impact on the nonbeliever. No amount of evangelizing or moralizing reaches as deep as the demonstration of love, forgiveness, and acceptance born of an identity that is firmly established in Christ

By allowing Christ to change the way we see ourselves—that we are His reflection and that we should see others through Him—we may be moved and renewed by that same love and concern. When we allow Christ to inform our actions and our feelings towards nonbelievers, we will indeed be able to demonstrate genuine respect and acceptance. Only then will others be willing to listen; this does not imply that by respecting them we are in agreement with conflicting views or that we abdicate our faith. Let's look at the example of the apostle Paul.

"So Paul, standing in the midst of the Areopagus, said: 'Men of Athens, I perceive that in every way you are very religious. For as I passed along and observed the objects of your worship, I found also an altar with this inscription, 'To the unknown god.' What therefore you worship as unknown, this I proclaim to you'" (Acts 17:22–23, ESV).

In his interactions with the Greeks, Paul used rhetoric, as was common in that day. Paul could have blasted the Athenians with condemnation of their idols, challenging the gods of the Greeks and calling the Greeks pagans. Instead he held their attention by saying that they were very religious. He did not alienate his listeners, but by being respectful he was given the opportunity to speak and for them to draw their own conclusions. When Paul addressed those outside the household of faith, he did so with simplicity and Greek reasoning so that listeners could understand his message.

On the other hand, Paul's tone in his epistles to the believers was quite different; there he encouraged, exhorted, or rebuked. They had already received the good news and were expected to walk in obedience to God. As their spiritual shepherd, Paul was responsible for the spiritual growth and walk of the Christians in Corinth, Thessalonica, Rome, and so on.

Much the same way, we should allow those who differ with our faith or worldview to express their views and even to condemn us. We can request equal time when we wish to tell the story of Jesus or when we desire to set the record straight. It is very difficult for someone to refuse to listen after we have first respectfully and silently listened; equal time in such a case is almost always readily granted.

"Let your gentleness be known to all men. The Lord is at hand" (Philippians 4:5, NKJV; some translations say "your reasonableness"). Because the Lord is near, we are admonished to be gentle or reasonable so that people can experience from our actions whom we serve and give them reason for pause, especially as Christ is near and time is of the essence. When Paul exhorted, "Let your gentleness be known," he meant for us to treat the other with kindness and consideration for Christ's sake and for the sake of God's kingdom. It is interacting in that spirit of gentleness, along with a genuine love and care for others, that attracts people to Christ.

There is nothing more exciting than being set ablaze by God's love. When we allow Jesus to help us deal with our idols, He transforms us and renews our minds through His Holy Spirit. We become so alive that our senses are heightened to everything around us. As we rediscover and live through God's perspective, we see what He sees; we live out love, compassion, and faith, and spread God's reconciliation wherever we are and wherever we go. In His love and power, and awakened from our apathy, we are ready to stand strong in our Christian faith; more importantly, in Christ we grow able to hold fast in the face of an increasingly hostile world that seeks to destroy Christians and their Christ.

As the following story testifies, we serve a great God, a living, powerful God, through whom we can move mountains!

Rocío's and Edison's Stories
[Translated from Spanish]

Edison arrived in Spain in March 2000, and his wife, Rocío, in March 2002; their children followed eight months after Rocío. They are from Ecuador and were forced to immigrate to Spain to escape the economic crisis in Ecuador. They went to look for greater economic stability in Spain.

God tells us in the midst of trials and tribulations He is with us, and if everything goes smoothly, then we should worry that He is not with us, and without our God we are nothing and are worth nothing.

To come to Spain was God's desire, as nobody in my country wanted me to go; all were against it, and even I had no wish to go. My husband was already in Spain; I did not wish to leave my parents or my children. It was very hard for me, but when my father died, I felt a great emptiness and loss. When my husband called, I said, "Edi, send for me." He became very excited and arranged for my travel, which all of my family members opposed.

My church, my family, and friends all said that this was not of God that I should travel. Nevertheless, one Sunday, in the early hours, the Lord spoke to me through His Word: "Be strong and courageous. Do not fear or be in dread of them, for it is the Lord your God who goes with you. He will not leave you or forsake you" (Deuteronomy 31:6–8, ESV). Another time He said: "I will go before you."

As I started to prepare the documents for my children, the opposition grew. People would prophesy and say: "If you go to Spain, the Lord will take away a son," and I would reply, "My children are not mine but the Lord's; therefore, nobody would be able to take my life or my husband's, and should he or I die, nobody would take anyone away, for we all belong to the Lord."

My brother said, "Look at that dog with her litter; not even dogs abandon their young!" Then the Holy Spirit gave me a word, and I told my brother, "In Jesus' name, this very year my children will be together with us." They thought I was out of my mind, but God willed it so. Seven months after I arrived in Spain, my children joined us, as did my three-month-old grandson; they were eight in all.

I thank God, who brought us to a good land and a good church founded and pastored by Pastor José Parraga. He was a man of God, full of love. He loved us and looked after us. He ensured that we lacked nothing, which in turn increased my love and faith for God. Pastor José watched out for all the foreigners; he was like a father and grandfather to us. Today He is in the Lord's presence, and we give thanks to God for sound scriptural doctrine he left as legacy.

Edison went first to Spain alone. There was much work available, but he did not have a contract that would have given him the right to work freely. The same year of his arrival, he was in a car accident in an overloaded van that carried fourteen passengers instead of nine. The driver drove through a railroad crossing without stopping for the oncoming train, and thirteen people died. All of them were illegal immigrants, and as a result of that accident the government found out how businessmen hired workers to work the land without following the legal requirements. The workers were not given any contract or social security. The immigration authorities and the police started sweeping checks, which made it the more difficult for foreigners to find work.

In September 2000 a construction company offered Edison a contract, which granted him Spanish residency and the right to work in the country. From that time on things changed for the better.

Edison shares:

It is not easy to travel so far, especially when leaving wife and children behind. I undertook the trip not knowing what was in store. I only trusted God, as I still do to this day. We went through many trials and difficulties and through it all learned not to despair. God is my help and my protection; He watches over my life and no one can touch it. Should any wish me harm, the worst that could happen is that they could take my life, which I consider gain.

Some people say they have gone through the desert. I'm here to say that I've already crossed the Jordan and am no longer in the desert. What remains of my old life is just as when Joshua drove out the pagan nations; likewise, I drive out, for example, lack of faith or any doubt, anger, or resentment that I may experience or that might be present in me.

It was near impossible for seven children and a nephew to make the trip together, as the flight ticket was very expensive. To our thinking it was impossible that they all come at once; at the same time, if we chose that each would travel separately, we were faced with the impossible dilemma of whom to choose first, and whom next, and so on. All wanted to be the first to go. God, however, is the expert in impossibilities.

One Saturday I went to install wooden flooring in a home. The owner was home, and we chatted about various topics. He then broached the subject of my conditions in Spain and of any children left behind in Ecuador. He asked me, "How are you planning to get your children over?" I replied, "If one doesn't have a godfather, he can't be baptized." Five minutes into the conversation the owner said, "I'm a bank manager at one of the branches of the Caja Murcia [a savings bank]. Why don't you come by my office next Monday, and we'll continue the conversation."

That following Monday the man told me, "I'll give you a loan so that you can bring your children over, but you'll have to find a guarantor." Since I was a foreigner, I didn't know any person or have a friend who could be my guarantor. I asked my employer, who had known me for one and a half years, but he declined, and so did another person whom I talked to.

One Saturday after church, as my wife and I prepared to go home, we were approached by a brother who asked how we were doing and when we would send for our children. We shared the situation with him, and then he said: "Don't bother looking for a guarantor, for here in front of you is one."

Our loan was then approved, but what was amazing is that this took place before I acquired my Spanish residence permit. The miracle lies in the fact that I didn't have any Spanish documents, without which it is impossible to obtain any loan, let alone a loan of 10,000 euros. This sum facilitated the travels of our twenty-year-old daughter and of six sons between the ages of three months (our nephew) and fifteen years. Thus came to pass what my wife had said to her brother: "In the name of Jesus, this same year all my children will be with us in Spain." Alleleuia! God, you are an incredible God!

For the last twelve years I've been worshiping at Bethel Evangelical Church in Sangonera la Seca (Murcia). And it has been three years since the death of Pastor José Párraga. Ismael, his son, is now pastoring the church. His father left very big shoes to fill. Many people in the church [who want to see change] have grown impatient, and so they can't understand Ismael, because they want to see his father in him. But Ismael is not Joseph; he is Ismael. And the impatience of the people obscures what God wants to do through him. However, the work is God's work and not that of men, and God will slowly realize his plans in every believer of this congregation.

A passage I read twenty years ago has helped me a lot; it was, it seems, a suggestion that had been given me specifically: "And you, Edison, my son, recognize the God of your fathers, and serve him with a perfect heart and a willing spirit; for the Lord searches the hearts of all and knows every intent of the heart. If you seek him, you will find him; but if you forsake him, he will cast you off forever." (1 Corinthians 28:10) This passage I also dedicated to my children.

"I do not nullify the grace of God"; "I have been crucified with Christ. It is no longer I who live, but Christ who lives in me. And the life I now live in the flesh I live by faith in the Son of God, who loved me and gave himself for me" (Galatians 2:21, 20, ESV).

As a Christian, I too am crucified with him, die with him and rise with him. All the old things in my life are, as it were, crucified with him and died with him; I am now a new creature in him. Therefore, I don't live as I lived before; I now live by letting Christ live in me, and Christ works in me what he wants. Since his nature is not capricious, Christ does his will in me because that is what is best for me.

The Lord gives each a measure of faith, which either grows or stops growing according to how each exercises his or her faith. Faith is not lacking but can be hidden or blocked.

There are some tests that seem very difficult to overcome; it seems that the Lord tarries in answering our prayers at such times. It may seem that months, even years, go by before the Lord answers, but the truth is that not a single day has gone by. Since for God a thousand years is as one day, that day has not yet finished. I tell my brothers and sisters who are being tested to take heart and not faint; there is still time. The Lord stands ready to help us.

Therefore, this is what Jehovah said: "If you return, I will restore you, and you shall stand before me.

"If you utter what is precious, and not what is worthless, you shall be as my mouth. They shall turn to you, but you shall not turn to them" (Jeremiah 15:19, ESV).

Lord Jesus, thank you for wanting to be my brother. Now you are also my Saviour and my Lord. I love you, Jesus; you are awesome!

Contact Information

To contact the author, or to arrange for workshops and speaking engagements, fill in the online contact form at www.writingsphinx.com.

BIBLIOGRAPHY

Barcus, Nancy B. *Developing a Christian Mind: A Fearless, Happy Ease amid the Conflicts of Secular Thought.* Downers Grove, Ill.: InterVarsity Press, 1979.

Goddard, Andrew D. *Jacques Elul on Idolatry.* Quoted in Stephen C. Barton ed. *Idolatry: False Worship in the Bible, Early Judaism and Christianity.* London and New York: T & T Clark, 2007.

Battle, Michael. *Practicing Reconciliation in a Violent World.* Harrisburg, Penn.: Morehouse, 2005.

Bonhoeffer, Dietrich. *The Cost of Discipleship.* New York: Macmillan,1963 rev. ed.

Brasher, Brenda E. *Give Me That Online Religion.* San Francisco: Jossey-Bass, 2001.

Clapp, Rodney, ed. *The Consuming Passion: Christianity and the Consumer Culture.* Downers Grove, Ill.: InterVarsity Press, 1997.

Dawson, Lorne L., and Douglas E. Cowan, eds. *Religion Online: Finding Faith on the Internet.* New York and London: Routledge, 2004.

Dickau, Tim. *Plunging into the Kingdom Way: Practicing the Shared Strokes of Community, Hospitality, Justice, and Confession.* Eugene, Oreg.: Cascade Books, 2010.

Goudzwaard, Bob. *Idols of Our Time.* Translated by Mark Van der Vennen. Foreword by Howard A. Snyder. Downers Grove, Ill.: InterVarsity Press, 1984.

Guinness, Os, and John D. Seel Jr., eds. *No God But God. Breaking with the Idols of our Age.* Chicago: Moody Press, 1992.

Mackay, Donald M. *The Clock Work Image.* Downers Grove, Ill.: InterVarsity Press, 1974.

Leibholz, Gerhard. *Memoir.* Quoted in Dietrich Bonhoeffer, *The Cost of Discipleship.* New York: Macmillan, 1963 rev. ed.

Morello, Carol. "Muslim Americans Say Life Is More Difficult since 9/11." *Washington Post,* August 30, 2011. *http://www. washingtonpost.com/local/muslim-americans-say-life-is-more-difficult-since-911/2011/08/29/gIQA7W8foJ_story.html.* Accessed May 11, 2012.

Newbegin, Lesslie. *The Gospel in a Pluralist Society.* Grand Rapids, Mich.: William B. Eerdmans, 1989.

Pew Research Center for the People & the Press. *"Muslim Americans: No Sign of Growth in Alienation or Support for Extremism. Mainstream and Moderate Attitudes - Section 1: A Demographic Portrait of Muslim Americans."* August 30, 2011. *http://www. people-press.org/2011/08/30/section-1-a-demographic-portrait-of-muslim-americans.* Accessed February 2012. *http://www.people-press.org/2011/08/30/muslim-americans-no-signs-of-growth-in-alienation-or-support-for-extremism.* Accessed March, 2011.

Pew Research Center. Internet & American Life Project. "The Social Side of the Internet." January 18, 2011. *http://pewinternet.org/Reports/2011/ The-Social-Side-of-the-Internet.aspx.* Accessed March 25, 2011.

Pew Research Center. Internet & American Life Project and Elon University Imagine the Internet: "Millennials will benefit and suffer due to their hyperconnected lives." February 29, 2012. *http://www.elon.edu/docs/eweb/predictions/expertsurveys/2012survey/ PIP_Future_of_Internet_2012_Gen_Always_ON.pdf.* Accessed May, 2012.

Pew Research Center. Religion & Public Life Project: *"Muslim Networks and Movements in Europe."* September 15, 2010. *http://www. pewforum.org/2010/09/15/muslim-networks-and-movements-in-western-europe/#text1.* Accessed March 2011.

Postman, Neil. *Amusing Ourselves to Death: Public Discourse in the Age of Show Business.* Viking Penguin, 1985.

Roy, Paul S.J. *Building Christian Communities for Justice: The Faith Experience Book.* New York: Paulist Press, 1981.

Schultze, Quentin J. *Habits of the High-Tech Heart: Living Virtuously in the Information Age.* Foreword by Jean Bethke Elshtain. Grand Rapids, Mich.: Baker Academic, 2002.

Z. Chris, "Freedom from E-mail", *The Plough Magazine,* 57 (Autumn 1998).

ENDNOTES

1   *No God But God. Breaking with the Idols of our Age.* Os Guinness, John D. Seel Jr. Editors, Richard Keyes, et al. (Moody Press, Chicago, Ill: 1992), 13.

2   Ibid.32–33.

3   Ibid. 33.

4   Ibid.

5   Dietrich Bonhoeffer in a letter to his friend Eberhard Bethge, 1944.

6   Ibid. 117.

7   Bob Goudzwaard, *Idols of Our Time* (Downers Grove, Ill.: InterVarsity Press, 1984), 13.

8   Tim Dickau, *Plunging into the Kingdom Way: Practicing the Shared Strokes of Community, Hospitality, Justice, and Confession.* (Eugene, Oreg.: Cascade Books, 2010), quoting Quentin Schultze, *Habits of the High-Tech Heart,* 183. Used by permission of Wipf and Stock. www.wipfandstock.com.

9   Lee Rainie, Kristen Purcell and Aaron Smith, Pew Research Center. Internet & American Life Project, *The Social Side of the Internet,* 1/18/2011 found that in the twelve months preceding their survey:

   • 22% of all adults (representing 28% of Internet users) signed up to receive alerts about local issues (such as traffic, school events, weather warnings, or crime alerts) via email or text messaging.

   • 20% of all adults (27% of internet users) used digital tools to talk to their neighbors and keep informed about community issues.. Overall, physical personal encounters remain the primary way people stay informed about community issues. In the twelve months preceding their survey:

   • 46% of Americans talked face-to-face with neighbors about community issues

   • 21% discussed community issues over the telephone

   • 11% read a blog dealing with community issues

   • 9% exchanged emails with neighbors about community issues, and 5% said they belong to a community email listserv

   • 4% communicated with neighbors by text messaging on cell phones

   • 4% joined a social network site group connected to community issues

- 2% followed neighbors using Twitter
http://pewinternet.org/Reports/2011/The-Social-Side-of-the-Internet.aspx. January 18, 2011.

[10] Janna Quitney Anderson, Elon University, Lee Rainie, Pew Research Center's Internet & American Life Project. "Millennials will benefit and suffer due to their hyperconnected lives" 2,7. "These findings come from an opt-in, online survey of a diverse but non-random sample of 1,021 technology stakeholders and critics. The study was fielded by the Pew Research Center, Internet & American Life Project and Elon University's Imagining the Internet Center, over a period from August 28 to October 31, 2011" p 7. http://www.elon.edu/docs/eweb/predictions/expertsurveys/2012survey/ PIP_Future_of_Internet_2012_Gen_Always_ON.pdf. Accessed May, 2012.

[11] Carol Morello, "Muslim Americans Say Life Is More Difficult since 9/11," *Washington Post*, August 30, 2011; http://www.washingtonpost.com/ local/muslim-americans-say-life-is-more-difficult-since-911/2011/08/29/ gIQA7W8foJ_story.html, accessed May 11, 2012.

[12] Pew Research Center for the People & the Press, " Muslim Americans: No Signs of Growth in Alienation or Support for Extremism" August 30, 2011, *http://www.people-press.org/2011/08/30/ muslim-americans-no-signs-of-growth-in-alienation-or-support-for-extremism.*

[13] Wiccans: Old English for witches. Druids: priests and magicians in ancient Celtic religions. Present-day Druids claim to be descendants of their descendants; Shamans: mostly in North American; while in a trance they connect with the spirit world and have the power to practise divination and healings. Sacred ecologists: whose roots are in Northern Canada, defined as a deep knowing of the sacredness of the earth, the interrelation between body and environment. Odinists: practise a form of neo-paganism by worshipping Odin and other Norse deities

[14] Atheism is the absence of belief in any gods, from the Greek *atheos*, "without God."

[15] Humanism stresses the importance of humans over the divine.

[16] Secularism can be defined by activities without spiritual basis.

[17] Rationalism sees actions based only on reason and facts, not on religious principles.

[18] For postmodernism there are no absolute truths; it rejects accepted principles and practices of its predecessor, modernism.

[19] Unitarian Universalism is a liberal religion that promotes a "free and responsible search for truth and meaning."

[20] Pew Center for the People and the Press, "Muslim Americans: No Sign of Growth in Alienation or Support for Extremism. Mainstream and Moderate Attitudes - Section 1: A Demographic Portrait of Muslim Americans" http://

www.people-press.org/2011/08/30/section-1-a-demographic-portrait-of-muslim-americans, accessed February 2012.

21 Pew Research Center. Religion & Public Life Project, "Muslim Networks and Movements in Europe," September 15, 2010; *http://www.pewforum.org/2010/09/15/muslim-networks-and-movements-in-western-europe/#text1*, accessed March 2011.

22 Brenda E. Brasher, *Give Me That Online Religion*. (San Francisco: Jossey-Bass,2001), 6–7.

23 Dietrich Bonhoeffer, *The Cost of Discipleship*. (New York: Macmillan, 1963).

24 *No God But God. Breaking with the Idols of our Age*. Os Guinness, John D. Seel Jr. Editors, Richard Keyes, et al. (Moody Press, Chicago, Ill: 1992). Used by permission,

25 Chris Z. "Freedom from E-mail," *The Plough Magazine* –Autumn 1998, Issue No 57, p.6. (Walden : The Plough, 1998), strikethrough and emphasis by Chris Z.

26 *Habit of the High Tech Heart.Living Virtuously in the Information Age*. Quentin J. Schultze. Foreword by Jean Bethke Elshtian.(Grand Rapids, Mich.: Baker Academic, 2002) 85-6.

27 Ibid. 117.

28 Ibid. 171-2.

29 These very laws remove the sense that one is obligated to be at a company's or business's beck and call at all hours of the day and night. British Columbia's Labour Law, for instance, states that minimum lunch breaks of thirty minutes are required and that if a person has to be available to work, then the company must pay for the break—which most companies do not, and therefore the worker is not obligated to be on call. It is therefore really up to the individual to decide whether to give in to that pressured need to be constantly available.

30 Shania Twain, "Ka-Ching!" ©Universal Music, November 19, 2002.

31 Bob Goudzwaard, *Idols of Our Time* (Downers Grove, Ill.: InterVarsity Press, 1984) 14.

32 *No God But God. Breaking with the Idols of our Age*. Os Guinness, John D. Seel Jr. Editors, Richard Keyes, et al. (Moody Press, Chicago, Ill: 1992)), 168-9. Used by permission .

33 Ibid. 66-7. Used by permission.

34 Ibid. 174. Used by permission.

35 Craig M. Gay, *Sensualists without Heart* as quoted by Rodney Clapp, ed. in *The Consuming Passion. Christianity and the Consumer Culture*, (Downers Grove, Ill.: InterVarsity Press, 1998) 38-9.

36 Jacques Ellul, *Ethics of Freedom* 159, as quoted by Andrew Goddard in *Jaques Ellul on Idolatry*. Stephen C. Barton, Editor. *Idolatry. False Worship in the Bible, Early Judaism and Christianity*. (London and New York: T&T Clark, 2007) 243, emphasis mine.

37   Neil Postman, *Amusing Ourselves to Death. Public Discourse in the Age of Show Business.* (New York: Viking Penguin,1985) 119-20.

38   Ibid. 3-4.

39   Tim Dickau, *Plunging into the Kingdom Way: Practicing the Shared Strokes of Community, Hospitality, Justice, and Confession.*, (Eugene, Oreg.: Cascade Books, 2010), 105. Used by permission of Wipf and Stock . www.wipfandstock.com

40   *Cost of Discipleship* [?]1935.

41   Dietrich Bonhoeffer, *The Cost of Discipleship,* (New York: Macmillan Publishers, 1963), 54, emphasis mine.

42   Gerhard Leibholz, *Memoir*, quoted in Dietrich Bonhoeffer, *The Cost of Disciplaship* rev. ed. (New York: Macmillan, 1963), 31.

43   Dietrich Bonhoeffer, *The Cost of Disciplaship* rev. ed. (New York : Macmillan, 1963), 63.

44   Bob Goudzwaard, *Idols of Our Time* (Downers Grove, Ill.: InterVarsity Press, 1984), 99-100.

45   *No God But God. Breaking with the Idols of our Age.* Os Guinness, John D. Seel Jr. Editors, Richard Keyes, et al. (Moody Press, Chicago, Ill: 1992)), 32. Used by permission.

46   Lesslie Newbegin, *The Gospel in a Pluralistic Society* (Grand Rapids, Mich.: William B. Eerdmans, 1989), 151.

47   Tim Dickau, *Plunging into the Kingdom Way: Practicing the Shared Strokes of Community, Hospitality, Justice, and Confession.*, (Eugene, Oreg.: Cascade Books, 2010), 104. Used by permission of Wipf and Stock Publishers, www. wipfandstock.com

48   Michael Battle, *Practicing Reconciliation in a Violent World,* (Harrisburg, Penn.: Morehouse, 2005), 49. Used by permission of Church Publishers Inc. New York.

49   Paul Roy, S.J., *Building Christian Communities for Justice. The Faith Experience Book,* (New York : Paulist Press, 1981), 136.

50   Tim Dickau, *Plunging into the Kingdom Way: Practicing the Shared Strokes of Community, Hospitality, Justice, and Confession,* (Eugene, Oreg.: Cascade Books, 2010), 102-3. Used by permission of Wipf and Stock Publishers. www. wipfandstock.com

51   Johann Christoph Blumhardt (1805-1880) was the pastor of the village of Möttlingen, in southern Germany. He helped free a young Christian woman, Gottliebin Dittus, from the bonds that the powers of darkness had kept her in. The struggle to set her free lasted almost two years. In the end, the demons attacked this Gottliebin's blind sister Katherine. Pastor Blumhardt would continue to alternately pray quietly and read Scripture aloud. At last, the last demon to be exorcised yelled, "Jesus is the Victor". After these events, a large-scale revival took place in the entire region, manifested by conversions and healings. Pastor Blumhardt, in his gentle manner, would continually direct

people to Christ as the only one who could free, save and heal. He would plainly state that only Jesus was the Victor over all the powers of darkness. The phrase, "Jesus is the Victor" would be used as an ongoing reminder of Christ's power, and was later adopted by Blumhardt's son, Christoph Friedrich Blumhardt.

[52] Lesslie Newbegin, *The Gospel in a Pluralistic Society*, (Grand Rapids, Mich.: William B. Eerdmans, 1989), 178.

[53] Tim Dickau, *Plunging into the Kingdom Way: Practicing the Shared Strokes of Community, Hospitality, Justice, and Confession*. (Eugene, Oreg.: Cascade Books, 2010), 101. Used by permission of Wipf and Stock Publishers. www. wipfandstock.com

[54] Ibid. 43. Used by permission of Wipf and Stock Publishers. www. wipfandstock.com

[55] Ibid. 101 – According to Exodus 20: -25. Used by permission of Wipf and Stock Publishers. www.wipfandstock.com

[56] Ibid. 108-10. Used by permission of Wipf and Stock Publishers. www. wipfandstock.com

[57] Ibid. 108. Used by permission of Wipf and Stock Publishers. www. wipfandstock.com

[58] Ibid. 108. Used by permission of Wipf and Stock Publishers. www. wipfandstock.com

[59] Michael Battle, *Practicing Reconciliation in a Violent World*, (Harrisburg, Penn.: Morehouse, 2005), 49-50. Used by permission of Church Publishers Inc. New York.

[60] Ibid. 99. Used by permission of Church Publishing Inc. New York.

[61] Tim Dickau, *Plunging into the Kingdom Way: Practicing the Shared Strokes of Community, Hospitality, Justice, and Confession*, (Eugene, Oreg.: Cascade Books, 2010), 38. Used by permission of Wipf and Stock Publishers. www. wipfandstock.com

[62] Paul Roy, S.J., *Building Christian Communities for Justice. The Faith Experience Book*, (New York : Paulist Press, 1981), 67

[63] Tim Dickau, *Plunging into the Kingdom Way: Practicing the Shared Strokes of Community, Hospitality, Justice, and Confession*, (Eugene, Oreg.: Cascade Books, 2010), 108. Used by permission of Wipf and Stock Publishers. www. wipfandstock.com

[64] Wilson-Hartgrove, *Beatitudes in the Desert*, 60, as quoted by Tim Dickau in *Plunging into the Kingdom Way: Practicing the Shared Strokes of Community, Hospitality, Justice, and Confession.*, (Eugene, Oreg.: Cascade Books, 2010), 134. Used by permission of Wipf and Stock Publishers. www.wipfandstock.com

[65] Paul Roy, S.J., *Building Christian Communities for Justice. The Faith Experience Book*, (New York : Paulist Press, 1981),113.

66 Ibid.182-3. Used by permission of Wipf and Stock Publishers. www. wipfandstock.com

67 Tim Dickau, *Plunging into the Kingdom Way: Practicing the Shared Strokes of Community, Hospitality, Justice, and Confession.*, (Eugene, Oreg.: Cascade Books, 2010), 45. Used by permission of Wipf and Stock Publishers. www. wipfandstock.com

68 Michael Battle, *Practicing Reconciliation in a Violent World*, (Harrisburg, Penn.: Morehouse, 2005), 48, 74. Used by permission of Church Publishing Inc. New York.

69 Tim Dickau, *Plunging into the Kingdom Way: Practicing the Shared Strokes of Community, Hospitality, Justice, and Confession.*, (Eugene, Oreg.: Cascade Books, 2010), 45. Used by permission of Wipf and Stock Publishers. www. wipfandstock.com

CPSIA information can be obtained at www.ICGtesting.com
Printed in the USA
LVOW12s0200131114

413387LV00001B/1/P